Number 8

Number 8

Mervyn Davies
with David Parry-Jones

foreword by John Dawes

 PELHAM BOOKS

First published in Great Britain by
PELHAM BOOKS LTD
52 Bedford Square, London WC1B 3EF
1977

© by Mervyn Davies and David Parry-Jones 1977

ISBN 0 7207 0980 6

Printed in Great Britain by Hollen Street Press Ltd at Slough
and bound by Redwood Burn Ltd, Esher, Surrey

Contents

Illustrations

The authors and publisher would like to thank the following for their kind permission to reproduce photographs: Aerpix Press (picture 5); *Evening Post*, Wellington, New Zealand (6); Topix (7, 9); *Western Mail and Echo* (8, 22); Colorsport (11a-d); Sport and General Press Agency Ltd (20, 21); London Express Pictures (23); Press Association Ltd (24); Thames Television (25).

The cartoon on pages 146-7 is reproduced by courtesy of Gren and the *South Wales Echo*.

Foreword

'There's a "number 8" playing for London Welsh 3rd XV who isn't much good but he's tall and can win some ball at the back of the line-out.' Those were the words of a junior selector at London Welsh at the end of October, 1968. Six matches later the same player – a certain Mervyn Davies – was awarded his first cap for Wales and went on to play thirty-eight consecutive games and contribute enormously to two very successful Lions tours.

Since his first cap Mervyn has travelled, either with Wales or the British Lions, to every major rugby-playing country in the world and in each he has been acclaimed not only as a world-class rugby player but probably the best ever in his position. To be asked therefore to write a foreword to his biography is a pleasure and privilege.

I have known Mervyn as a player, as his captain and more recently as his coach, and in every aspect the one quality which was always prominent was his total reliability. Seldom was it necessary to utter words of advice – rather to seek them, although those who know him will recognise immediately that he is a man of few words. Of his ability there can be no doubt, but the aspect of his play that continually surprised me even up until the Wales *v.* France game in 1976 was his fantastically high level of consistency. When one thinks of other great players one can recall an occasion when they had an 'off-day' – but no such comment is applicable to Mervyn. Even in the game mentioned above when Mervyn received an injury early during play which would have forced most players to retire, he still continued not only to play but to play to a very very high level. It would not be an understatement – nor disrespectful to his replacements — to say that had he not continued Wales would probably have lost the match.

Mervyn as a player and a captain was totally uncompromising but always played with great respect for his colleagues and his opponents. He had the quality as a captain to inspire, by personal example, properly channelled aggression into his pack of forwards, thereby producing games of memorable quality. It was ironic that the illness which forced his retirement should occur during a match when he was playing with or against five of his Wales comrades from his pack. Such is the respect for him that his opponents that day probably felt worse than anyone else in Wales. How thankful we all are that he is now on the way to recovery.

In writing this foreword, tribute must be paid to Mervyn's enormous contribution to the famous '71 and '74 Lions. Perhaps it is best summed up by saying that without any doubt he would have captained the 1977 British Lions to New Zealand — a decision which would have been unanimous with every rugby player and supporter.

Sadly, Mervyn has now given up playing rugby, but he still has much to contribute to the game. Above all else, when one has to name someone for young players to try and emulate it would be easy to mention other great names, especially the 'prima donnas' as Mervyn would say, but there can be no finer player than 'Merv the Swerve'. It only remains to say that I personally had the great fortune to play with him and even better luck not to play against him!

Mervyn, for your contribution to London Welsh, Wales, the British Lions and to rugby football in particular, I would like to say 'Thank you'.

John Dawes

Prologue: The Watershed

They were three princes of Welsh rugby, men of stature and ac-
quainted with victory: Bleddyn Williams, the outstanding midfield
player of the post-war game in Britain; Clem Thomas of the deep
chest and twinkling eye, once a ubiquitous and deadly flank
forward; and Brian Price, master of the line-out and a
recently retired Triple Crown captain.

But on this day their faces were long, their voices grave.

The date was April 1971 and the trio had come before the
television cameras one sunny morning at Cardiff Arms Park to sum-
marise prospects for the British Isles touring party which would
soon leave for New Zealand. And theirs was not a pretty prognosis.

Price, the end of his rugby career scarred by two savage Test
maulings during Wales's 1969 trip down under, spoke harrowingly
of All Black forward power and the might of men like Meads,
Kirkpatrick and Whiting. Thomas thought that the Lions would be
a tougher proposition than their predecessors of 1966, but nonetheless warned that the Test series was bound to be lost. Bleddyn
Williams, who had led a Wales XV which included Clem Thomas
to victory over the 1953 All Blacks in Britain, explained the New
Zealander's fanatical determination to win on his own soil, and concluded that this would swing the rubber decisively against the
British Isles.

The fact that they were proved wrong, and that John Dawes's
Lions became the first to win a full series in New Zealand, and only
the second touring side to return victorious since the game was first
played there, is irrelevant. More interesting in retrospect is their attitude: the belief that in competition the British were under-dogs,
doomed to gallant but inevitable defeat.

The story you are embarking upon is about the dramatic crossing of a watershed in the British approach to playing rugby football at the highest competitive levels, and about the contribution of one man in particular to that achievement.

As an attitude, sadly, defeatism has by no means been uncommon in British sport in recent decades — and indeed, many would argue that it is soundly based. If world-wide recognition is a criterion, then Britain's boxers, golfers, tennis players and athletes (including competitors participating in the broad spectrum of the Olympic Games) have with a very few noble exceptions failed to win top honours, and no knowledgeable critic would predict with confidence, or even hope, that better days are in the offing.

England's Association Football XI enjoyed an *annus mirabilis* in 1966, but subsequently the soccer wiseacres have fought shy of suggesting that the game in these islands is the best in the world, and that any of the British nations will win matches. It seems to be accepted that the cleverest and best organised sides are now to be found on the European mainland or in Latin America. In a rather more limited context, English cricket has not been notable for success stories.

And it has to be admitted that, during this century, the rugby teams of the home countries have experienced more than their fair share of failure at the hands of opponents from abroad, inexorably diminishing the expectations of those who cared deeply about the game. In competition with the two major exponents of rugby in the southern hemisphere, New Zealand and South Africa, British sides usually played second fiddle on the occasions that mattered. For instance, until 1971 South Africa had won thirty-seven Tests against Lions teams or individual national sides and lost but seven; New Zealand had won thirty-nine and lost six.

A trend in the same direction was discernible within Europe. After an absence from international fixtures during the thirties and the war years, it took the French a long time to mount challenges for supremacy in the Five Nations' Championship. But by the middle sixties their teams were flush with confidence, they were capturing championship titles, and Colombes had become an almost impregnable citadel. British observers looked with envy at their ebullient forward play with its sure-fingered catching and split-second passing wedded to Gallic inventiveness in midfield. It was fashionable to doff the hat to French flair and methods.

And so English, Scottish, Irish and Welsh rugby men, like their compatriots associated with other sports, had come to feel that defeat, especially at the hands of the great southern hemisphere nations, was a foregone conclusion, to be suffered as graciously and sportingly as possible. After a wry remark to the effect that 'We taught these chaps to play the game', the head was placed obediently on the block and the descent of the axe awaited. And at no time was the British neck more soft and pliant than in 1966, when M. J. Campbell-Lamerton's Lions toured New Zealand. His side contained some brilliant individuals; but because of off-the-field friction, uninspired captaincy and some extraordinary selection decisions, there is evidence to suggest that the Britons scarcely ever took the field with the feeling that they could win. Four Tests were lost; critics condemn it as the most disastrous tour of the century by any country; and a decade later it certainly looks like the absolute nadir.

Consider the contrast when, in autumn 1967, Brian Lochore's Sixth All Blacks came to Britain. Managed by the confident C. K. Saxton, they boasted a captain well worth his place. They walked tall and radiated an air of menacing assurance – which was shared, incidentally, by the whole party, Pressmen and all: the critic Terry McLean was interviewed on radio on the eve of the Test against Wales at Cardiff, only days after a West Wales XV had given the tourists a hard game before succumbing 21-14. When asked, however, to predict the result of the Test, McLean snapped out with not a moment's hesitation, 'Wales 6, the All Blacks 14' (the result was actually 6-13).

The New Zealanders also had with them Fred Allen, a man they referred to as a coach, not as an assistant manager. Clearly very much in charge of everything that did not bear directly on administration, at training sessions he exchanged blazer and flannels for a track suit, and huffed, puffed and perspired like one of his players. The team won all four of their representative matches in

Europe by comfortable margins; but more importantly they are remembered for playing attractive fifteen-man rugby and for running up nearly 300 points in fifteen matches.

As they moved around Britain they still found the traditional deference accorded to them. Host clubs still told them self-deprecatingly, 'We hope to give you a good game, but ...' Newspaper headlines still forecast, 'England need a miracle this afternoon,' or 'New Zealand to win – but Wales could run them close.' Reporters continued to speak and write of the 'ruck' as if it were some magical formula injected into the play by colonial witch-doctors, incapable of being grasped by hang-dog home teams. When the tourists left for home they were told, 'We'll be out to win in 1971,' but nobody really believed it, least of all the All Blacks themselves. When Wales, Triple Crown holders, were sunk without trace in 1969 it simply seemed confirmation: the British were losers, through and through.

And yet, imperceptibly, the tide had turned.

The West Wales XV referred to earlier had gone to unusual lengths in preparing for its match against Lochore's team. Its players, although drawn from four clubs, had actually practised together beforehand and talked long and earnestly about their approach to the play. The training and the conversations were directed by a former Welsh International stand-off half called Carwyn James. Later on, in the penultimate fixture of their British tour, the All Blacks were held to a draw by an East Wales XV which had also assembled beforehand and trained as a group under another former International, David Hayward – the measure of their achievement is the fact that, in 144 previous games in Europe at all levels, New Zealand sides had failed to win only thirteen. Their bacon was saved on this occasion by a late try from Steel – but the writing was on the roof of the grandstand: squads, and coaching, had arrived in Britain.

They were, as it has emerged, symptomatic of a change of attitude that was to be total and which has arguably set British rugby apart from other sports. It has not been brought about without enormous deliberation and constructive thinking.

For years rugby men in the home countries had felt that there was little wrong with the calibre of individual players produced by their system. Yet when united into teams and pitted against the sternest opposition they but rarely obtained the desired results. The men who shared the 1955 Test series 2-2 in South Africa were fêted on their return as if they had conquered the world, and indeed they had done better than earlier generations. Yet in truth their achievement was narrowly to avoid defeat. Why, though, had they failed to win – with players who were giants in their own right like Cliff Morgan, O'Reilly, Butterfield, Jeeps, McLeod, Rhys Williams and the captain Robin Thompson?

The Welsh, whose belief in the near-divinity of their own players is profound if at times rather touching, puzzled over the riddle more doggedly than most. Wales's rugby geography is neat and compact, making for deep companionship and a closer relationship among the rugby fraternity than in any other country: if you wish to be in bed in Llanelli by 2 am you do not need to forsake congenial company in Cardiff until well after midnight. So the tongues wagged more vigorously than elsewhere and much midnight oil flickered and ran dry.

The hunt for answers had reached fever pitch in 1963 after a hopeful Welsh expedition had paid a short visit to South Africa and lost a Test match by 24-3. It was a national calamity; but the long, arduous think-tank seminars which followed it convinced the Welsh Rugby Union that salvation must lie in organisation, preparation and method.

The logic was elementary and direct: since winning was the object of the game and to lose, especially heavily, left an unfulfilled feeling near the pit of the stomach, Welsh rugby had to get better. Since rugby is a team game, teams must be better. How best to improve them? By increasing their fitness, their skills and their cohesion in ploys and tactics. Could this be effected by admonition and stern lectures? Given the average fun-loving, beer-swigging amateur rugby player, it was most unlikely. How, then? Answer: by appointing ring-masters to crack the whip and insist upon application and endeavour. Clubs must appoint coaches (the national XV would have one too, and the WRU would even appoint an executive to supervise the innovations).

What would coaches do? They would engender confidence by talking of success and glory. They would plot victories, not the avoidance of defeat. They would make demands on individual players' skill and effort, and would foster team-spirit and team-work. And they would inspire their men.

It is not the role of this Prologue to discuss the furore that such edicts brought in their train or the reluctance of many clubs to do as they were bidden. Suffice to say that after the introduction of total coaching in 1968 and the appointment of Clive Rowlands as national XV coach, Wales won five outright championship titles in eight winters, with three Triple Crowns and two Grand Slams. In addition, properly coached British sides overseas have come through with flying colours, first in New Zealand and then in South Africa. The other United Kingdom countries have not yet embraced the coaching ideal so fondly as Wales (indeed there are good reasons why they cannot); but they too have enjoyed days of consummate achievement, notably England with her tremendous victories in Auckland and Johannesburg.

Coaches and squads, then, are both the symptoms of British rugby's confident new attitude to the game and, by now, agents in perpetuating it. Ray Williams, the coaching organiser appointed by the WRU in 1968, believes that we are metaphorically light years away from the time when an international XV would assemble in its dressing room an hour before the kick-off so that its captain could ascertain the names of the new caps. The British game has entered a new era — arguably its greatest.

Two other points remain to be dealt with. The first is connected with the quality of the rugby game, as an exercise for players and as a spectacle for onlookers.

It is hard for the young reader of today, accustomed to flowing, rippling tides of attacking rugby, to imagine how shatteringly dull the game could be until the late sixties. Those were days when forwards wrestled and mauled for the ball (or, worse still, lay on it) without the faintest intention of releasing it for others to have fun with. Their numbing lack of finesse was, with some noble exceptions, shared by inside backs, whose first instinct after a line-out was to kick the ball back into touch. Wales once won a game at

Murrayfield when the ball went out of play 121 times. The type of stand-off half considered to be a match-winner was Mike Weston of England, who kept his centres on a starvation diet but could punt the ball a mighty long way.

The full-back was confined to the rear of the play. His principal task was to field kicks ahead safely and accurately before putting the ball back into touch, with a minimum of delay and a territorial gain if possible. He was expected to be a sound tackler, but speed and mobility were correspondingly lower priorities. Cardiff's Frank Trott was a classic example of the species: a full-back with nine virtues out of ten, but if he had only possessed the speed to catch Ochse at the corner flag his club would have lowered the colours of the 1950 Springboks instead of losing 11-9 through the South African wing's late try. Bob Scott, who toured Britain with the 1953-4 All Blacks was admired but written off as an eccentric individualist when he actually carried the ball forward from full-back to link with the midfield backs, and of course he was years ahead of his time. But Scott had another skill which full-backs of the day were expected to cultivate – he kicked goals (and could do so in bare feet).

Back-row forwards in the pre-1968 era were marauders supreme, and they contributed to the negative thinking of all but the best backs by lying up on opposing midfield triangles or creeping round the scrum to harass scrum-halves. Big, fast number 8 forwards like Muller and Hopwood were excellent exploiters of the latitude permitted by the laws of the day and, like England's Peter Robbins, were frustrators of free-ranging, running rugby behind the scrum. Backs such as Cliff Morgan and Richard Sharp could sometimes beat the system, but their opportunities, particularly at representative level, were pitifully few.

The net result of factors like these was that tries were relatively rare occurrences, and since its main aim is the carrying of the ball across the line, the game was inevitably far less entertaining, if tenser, than it is today. Sometimes isolated International matches would burst into bloom, but usually because one side was considerably superior to its opponents. When all things were equal, a war of attrition was the commonest outcome.

Then, coincidentally with the introduction of coaching to rugby in the British Isles, Australia successfully advocated her 'dispensation rule' before the International Board, rugby's law-making body. Kicking to touch on the full between the 22-metre lines was forbidden, or 'dispensed with'. At one stroke the move altered the whole emphasis of the game in the direction of handling. It was perhaps the biggest fillip to the rugby code since William Webb Ellis's historic piece of enterprise.

It meant that backs were deprived of the easy option. Under great pressure, close to their own line, they could still use the touch-finder, but in all other situations their first thought had to be about handling the ball and running with it. The skip-kick to touch might still be employed (and the top players soon acquired mastery of it), and so could an up-and-under, but both required considerable judgement and accuracy lest the opposition should reply with interest.

Full-backs, in particular, needed to re-think their role, which had traditionally been to find touch; and after discovering novel, exciting ways of linking with the three-quarters in front of them their appetite for action was whetted, and they began to seek constant involvement in attacking moves. Imaginative men like J. P. R. Williams, entering the line judiciously, realised that they could convert themselves from pure defenders into potent and high-scoring attackers.

Other legal reforms adjusted the line of advantage in favour of backs and made handling slightly easier, improving the flow of play. But it was the permanent adoption of the Australian rule which cleared the decks for rugby union football to begin realising its full potential for entertainment, both to watch and to play. Its rhythm used to be stop-start, comparing unfavourably with what seemed to be perpetual motion in the rival handling code, rugby league football. Now the studs are on the other boot.

Thus conditions had been created whereby a new, dynamic kind of rugby could be played, while the coaching revolution had already begun to throw up men of character and vision who were determined that it should. The stage was set, the directors were eager; where were the players?

Whether cause and effect played a part or whether it was all coincidence is not yet easy to decide. The fact is that a crop of truly outstanding men swiftly emerged to grace the rugby of the late sixties and seventies by exploiting the new laws and the new spirit of the game to the full. They were to raise endeavour to new heights and give undreamed-of aesthetic pleasure by their sheer brilliance, at the same time combining as teams to blend the best of their separate abilities. Nor were they all players: the coaches, too, talked in accents that fell freshly on British ears. They spoke of success through beating the hide off opponents and, if possible, through high quality play; they had analytical minds which could devise methods of achieving their goal; and above all they could transmit ideas to the men they coached and fire them with ambition.

A number of them were Welsh. Carwyn James of the urbane manner and silver tongue espied and took his opportunity. John Dawes, on the field and as a coach, took his. Gareth Edwards, Gerald Davies, Barry John, Phil Bennett, J. P. R. Williams and John Taylor dazzled crowds and baffled opponents with performances that were often touched with genius. Ireland's warriors, too, like McBride, McLoughlin and Gibson enjoyed an Indian summer during which Syd Millar coached the 1974 Lions to immortality with an unbeaten tour of South Africa. England produced Duckham, as great a back as any in the world, and together with Scotland provided props and locks who were platforms for British rugby's new stance on top of the world.

There was another young man who stepped gingerly under the spotlight of representative rugby early in 1969. Born twenty-two years earlier he had sprouted to a height of 6 feet, $4\frac{1}{2}$ inches and packed $14\frac{1}{2}$ stones into a lean, spare frame. A member of the London Welsh club, he was virtually unknown in Wales, so that many an eyebrow was raised when the selectors chose him as their number 8 for the International campaign's opening match at Murrayfield. In a side which won 17-3 he played a careful game, taking care to fit into the Welsh scheme of things. He was never subsequently omitted by his country, or by the British Lions, for whom he was the Test number 8 on two major tours. In a period when the backs' appetite for the ball had been stimulated by new laws, he became an expert at providing it; and also a tough, ruthless initiator of constructive forward moves.

He has thus viewed at close quarters the entry of the British game into its new era, has contributed to its new assurance, and would be named by most observers the world over as one of the best two or three men ever to play in the number 8 position.

His name is Thomas Mervyn Davies, 'Merv the Swerve'.

1   *End Game*

David Parry-Jones

The fateful question had been put and the hospital board-room fell silent except for the whirr of television cameras. The pens of two dozen reporters from the world's Press hovered expectantly above their notebooks. Neuro-surgeon Robert Weeks drew a deep breath.

'Yes,' he agreed finally. 'You can say that. Mervyn Davies is fighting for his life.'

So that was it — end of Press conference. A sub-arachnoid or intra-cranial haemorrhage had tragically interrupted the career of a giant of world rugby and one of Wales's sporting heroes lay at death's door. Sadly but urgently the media men moved off to convey the grave news to the community at large, some of them reflecting how a mere twenty-four hours earlier everything in the Welsh rugby garden had been lovely.

Under Mervyn Davies's captaincy the national XV had just marched inexorably to its second European championship title on the trot, claiming a Grand Slam of four victories in the process. Domestically, the Challenge Cup competition was destined for a splendid climax with Llanelli, the cup-holders, already through to the final and now, on Sunday, 28 March 1976, a Swansea team who were also skippered by Merv the Swerve due to do battle with Pontypool at Cardiff Arms Park to decide who would meet them.

Few people thought it would be a spectacular match, since the emphasis would almost certainly be upon the forward struggle. Pontypool, although robbed by injury of a brilliant flanker and captain in Terry Cobner, put the current Welsh International front row on to the field — Faulkner, Windsor and Price — plus a Wales B lock, Floyd; Swansea's pack included full caps in Phil Llewellyn, Wheel,

Trevor Evans, Keyworth (of England) and Mervyn Davies himself, as well as another Wales B player, Clegg. The exchanges seemed certain to be robust — and they were. But they were also clean, as if the two eights had too much respect for each other to bother with dirty or underhand play.

For nearly half an hour, on perfect turf and under a bright spring heaven, the teams sparred away with neither able to gain a decisive advantage, and it was ironically in the events leading up to the All Whites' first try by Woodward that fate struck their captain down. He had taken part in a maul near the half-way line and been instrumental in winning possession for Swansea. He backed up as the attack moved to the right touch-line, before turning in the opposite direction when his side slipped the ball to the backs and the play switched towards the left, or open, side of the field.

It was as he sought to pick up speed and support the move that the big, tall number 8 suddenly pitched to the ground and lay prone. Nobody was near him at the time and nobody saw his fall, for all eyes were upon Swansea's backs, racing through for a magnificent try 60 yards distant near the left corner flag. His fourteen teammates were over the moon with delight and oblivious for the moment to everything else.

At length, however, the skipper's plight was seen and a stretcher swiftly borne out to him. Swansea's jubilation turned to dismay as their great champion was taken from the field, motionless and clearly unconscious. The remaining All Whites pulled out all the stops and won a fine victory eventually by 22 points to 14, but their joy at the final whistle was tempered by concern for the absentee. 'How is Merv?' everyone wanted to know. 'Where is he?' The most a grim-faced Swansea chairman Viv Davies could say was that the captain had failed to recover consciousness in the changing-room and had been taken from the ground by ambulance.

Things were blacker than anyone could have imagined. Mervyn had stopped breathing on the massage table and must have died had it not been for the availability of a resuscitator, which gave the mechanical equivalent of the kiss of life. The first doctors on the scene, Gordon Rowley, honorary surgeon to the WRU, and Jack Matthews, a GP who had won seventeen caps for Wales in the post-war years, lost no time in summoning an ambulance to rush him to Cardiff Royal Infirmary accompanied by his wife Shirley, whose pale-faced composure won their admiration.

At six o'clock Robert Weeks was alerted at his home by telephone and having absorbed the facts as given by the duty registrar, Dr Bob Leyshon, ordered that the patient should be moved to the area's newest and most lavishly equipped medical centre, the University of Wales Teaching Hospital at the Heath, where he saw him twice during the evening. The big fellow was paralysed down the left side of his body (though some strength returned to his hand overnight) and Dr Weeks deduced that he had suffered a haemorrhage within the brain. The following morning he dealt guardedly with questions at the Press conference, but he already suspected that a major operation would have to be undertaken the moment Mervyn Davies was strong enough.

That time came after a week. An arteriogram, which provides a cinematographic view of the passage of blood through the brain's arteries, and an isotope scan test had revealed the problem and the nature of the damage, and on 6 April Dr Weeks decided he must make the attempt to mend the weak artery. He needed to penetrate to a point three inches inside his patient's skull directly behind the bridge of the nose, and his object would be to isolate a vulnerable section of a blood-vessel wall. He likens the technique to clipping the neck of an inner tube which has swollen and bulged through the protecting wall of a rubber tyre.

It would be a delicate, intricate task, and Robert Weeks was all too aware of the glare of publicity focused upon his skill. He performed this kind of operation about once a week, always with the risk that a sufferer might subsequently die, and he well knew the degree of precision needed to disentangle the mesh of smaller arteries in order to expose and pin-point the exact area for attention. He would also have to ensure that the brain was not left liable to blood starvation, which could bring about a further collapse or a fatality.

This day, though, he and his team of seven rose to the challenge and did a thoroughly smooth, efficient job of work, so that three hours after they had begun Mervyn could be wheeled back to Ward

B4 to start convalescing. Seven or eight days later the neuro-surgeon decided cautiously that the operation had been a success and that the patient was out of danger. He felt the satisfaction of one whose expertise had met and passed a severe test. And although each and every one of his patients was equally important to him, as a follower of good rugby who had often seen Mervyn Davies playing for Wales, he felt especially glad to have been able to treat him.

The crisis was over, and bulletins on Merv's progress now no longer made front-page news. There were pictures of him – shorn of the unruly mop of dark, curly hair – and interviews began to be carried in the Press and on television. And in due course came the expected confirmation that the Welsh captain, his country's most capped forward, would not play rugby again. People had hoped against hope that his career could continue, but when the die was cast they felt relief that he was prudent enough not to tempt fate a second time.

They also felt sad. Since 1969 Mervyn Davies had been an ever-present in Welsh and British XVs that had enjoyed extra-ordinary success. An era had drawn to a close.

MERVYN DAVIES

Some people will call it a premonition; I sometimes think it was the build-up to the brain haemorrhage I was about to suffer. But the morning before what was to be my last competitive game of rugby football I felt lousy. It was almost as if I knew that some direful happening was about to befall me.

I never experienced nerves or hang-ups before matches, but that day, as the Swansea coach sped towards Cardiff Arms Park and our meeting with Pontypool in the Cup semi-final, the club captain was really out of sorts. At lunch in a Cowbridge hotel I toyed with my food; on arrival at Cardiff I vaguely remember discussing the weather conditions with Carwyn James without much enthusiasm – there was an annoying, gusty wind coming in over the Taff; and in the changing-room beforehand I can recall sprawling listlessly on a bench. I ought to have been relishing the prospect of clashing with Ray Prosser's well-drilled 'Pool pack: instead I moped.

Thereafter, I must confess, everything is a blank. I do not

remember the kick-off or any of the half-hour's play before I collaps-
ed. Onlookers say that I was not in a dominant mood — well, I have
to accept their word for it. For as far as I am concerned what
followed is a fortnight's gap in my consciousness — no pain, no discomfort, no dreadful trauma: just a lost fourteen days. That is a lot
of time out of anyone's life, especially when you're twenty-nine, ostensibly in your prime, and used to a non-stop round of positive living in vigorous, active company.

They did not show me the newspaper headlines which
trumpeted, 'Mervyn Davies fights for his life.' If they had I could
not have taken them in, for I retain only hazy impressions of my early days at the University of Wales Hospital after they had carried
me away from the Arms Park. Among the most vivid, oddly
enough, is of that very first evening, when I momentarily came to,
said to myself, 'What the hell am I doing here in bed?' and strug-
gled to my feet with my father and a couple of nurses trying to hold
me down. My legs, which had carried me across some of the
world's great rugby arenas without a twinge, bent under me like in-
dia-rubber and I sank back on to the bed and into oblivion.

What else? I recall splitting headaches, for which the nurses
declined to give me relieving tablets lest they should provoke
bleeding again within my head. Perhaps that is why my neuro-
surgeon Robert Weeks told reporters at a Press conference the morning after my collapse, 'He's awake, but he's in a foul temper'!
Faces loomed into my consciousness and faded away: my wife
Shirley, my father Dai (Betty, my mother, took on the job of looking after her little grandson Christopher and, perhaps fortunately,
could not come to see my condition for herself), and Dr John P. R.
Williams, who I believe smuggled in a few cans of ale which I was
unable to help him drink. I remember, too, a piece of paper which I
was asked to sign being pushed under my nose. I managed to scrib-
ble a wobbly signature: it was the permission medical authorities
require to carry out a major operation.

I am told that they would have liked more time for a more
thorough diagnosis, but in the end the risk of a second, fatal
bleeding became too acute, and it was 1 am on 6 April when Shirley
received a summons at our home in Pontlliw, Swansea, to say that

my condition was critical and the operation would take place later that morning. Although fact is now hard to distinguish from imaginings I believe that I was aware that part of my brain needed surgery if I was to live and that there was a chance that I might not pull through. Yet I do not remember experiencing fear: perhaps I was drugged into a state of euphoria, but I could say to myself through the mists, 'There are no two ways about it, Mervyn, you're going to live.' I might have been more cautious had I known that I would spend all morning on the operating table.

My bad tempers persisted after I emerged from the theatre, particularly as I was woken regularly each quarter-hour for my temperature and pulse to be taken. But I think that in the end the staff of B4 found me, if not a model patient, a co-operative one. Mind you, a little native cunning came in useful now and then: Sister Julia Morris had a horror of alcohol in the shape of beer imported by my friends, and I learned to trade a promise not to imbibe in exchange for an extra pillow or a few more moments in bed at reveille. I admit to being an easy-going, even lazy sort of guy, so the one thing I really disliked during my convalescence was physiotherapy. In retrospect the physios were wonderful, but at the time I hated their whole regime. They drove me hard – for my own good, of course – and did mean things like removing my bed-pan to make me walk to the lavatory.

The days lengthened as spring began giving way to summer, and they felt long too as my recovery, for which lots of rest and inactivity was vital, got under way. But there were compensations. My mail-bag was enormous and filled me with a sense of wonder and humility at the concern that was expressed for my return to health. I had some four thousand letters and cards, from all over Wales and the world, including one from a group of girls whom I had taught as eleven-year-olds in my first junior school at Mitchett in Surrey. I was well enough by then to reflect that by now they would be eighteen-year-olds and probably something special to look at! There was a letter from New Zealand's hooker, Tane Norton, accompanying a copy of a biography of his fellow countryman, Fergie McCormick, a controversial full-back. Willie John McBride wrote from Ireland, as did many friends in England, Scotland and France.

To the bulk of the correspondence I was in no physical state to reply, and was grateful to the BBC and some newspapers for allowing me to pass on a general thank you to well-wishers.

Once I was off the danger-list, about a fortnight after I had been laid low, the visitors began to call. Sometimes, inadvertently, they reminded me of how ill I had been and still was. John Dawes, my old London Welsh, Wales and British Lions mate, breezed in one day with Madora and Derek Quinnell, and with Sister's permission decided to give me my first breath of fresh air in the hospital grounds. Into a wheelchair I flopped and down we all went to the ground floor. But as the party moved gaily through long corridors to the sunshine I was suddenly overcome by immense fatigue and had to beg them to retrace our journey straight back to the ward.

Another day I received twenty-three visitors in one hour, which left me very limp. But I was genuinely glad to see people, especially callers like Barry John, Cliff Morgan, the WRU secretary Bill Clement and all five Welsh selectors. Later on, after my move to Gorseinon, West Wales friends could more readily drop in – Phil Bennett seemed to spare a few minutes almost every day. And since our home at Pontlliw was close by, my small son Christopher, aged one, could now be brought in. On his first visit he delighted me by walking into the ward – before my illness he had been a crawler!

When I finally left Gorseinon, stiff and with slightly blurred vision, but able to attend physiotherapy as an out-patient, there was one unforeseen penalty awaiting me at home: as a result of my ordeal my sense of smell had temporarily disappeared, so Shirley judged that I could now be the changer-in-chief of Christopher's nappies! Mind you, my wife has been a tower of strength throughout. She spent unending sleepless hours at my bedside in the critical days after my collapse, helped me to remain patient during the dull, empty days while I recovered strength, and after my return home insisted that I kept active without over-taxing myself. My father, too, was never far from my side, and it must have been one of the cigarettes which he regularly provided that I demanded the moment I came out of my post-operative coma. He and Shirley realise more clearly than I, I feel sure, how narrowly I cheated death.

Robert Weeks is a man for whom I have respect and gratitude. I admire his professional skill and know that had be been a millimetre in error the morning he operated on me, I should not be alive today. He also kept my morale high and never allowed me to doubt that I would eventually recover. He even tried to procure an outsize bed for his 6-foot-4½-inch patient, and when that failed they had to remove the end from a standard one!

So when, a week after the operation, he told me that I would be unwise to play rugby again I pricked up my ears. 'Remember, I am not absolutely forbidding you to,' he added, before padding away on his rounds. It was as his footsteps died away that I faced reality, recognised that he was talking sense, and made up my mind: enough was enough — it was time to call it a day.

Ever since the return of the British Lions from South Africa in 1974 I had told myself that if I suffered a serious injury, such as a bad fracture, I would retire. And to be honest, although I knew that there would be pressure on me from the likely coach John Dawes to accept the captaincy of the British Isles party bound for New Zealand in 1977, I had already decided to hang up my boots before the tour, at the end of the Home Championship season. My respect for All Black power is huge, I considered that it would be a hard campaign with no easy matches, and I didn't really want to know.

For almost all my ambitions in rugby had been fulfilled. I'd had two Lions tours, a host of International caps, and the captaincy of Wales with a culminating Grand Slam to add to earlier Triple Crown and title triumphs. The game had taken me all over the world — to Japan, China, Ceylon, Canada, the United States and the South Seas as well as Europe, South Africa and Australasia. I had become a Barbarian and seen my name join that of my father on the captains' role of honour at the Swansea club. I had, too, played in a great era of British rugby football and enjoyed every minute of it.

Moreover, there was no feeling that I owed the game anything. It had been my whole life for seven years, with only one summer free of an overseas tour since 1968. There were the hours spent playing, training, attending functions, speaking at dinners, opening fêtes in the name of sportsmanship. I felt that I was in credit, and that my private life and my family now deserved some consideration. And finally I knew no bitterness or resentment towards rugby at my condition, for I had been assured by the doctors that the haemorrhage could have occurred at any time and in any circumstances.

So the logic was inescapable and the decision, once made, not difficult to accept. As I lay in bed, though, occasionally flexing my weak left arm, I couldn't help casting my mind over the things about the game that I would miss. No more the ultra-intimate companionship, born of competing and competition and nurtured in changing-rooms before and after a match. No more limelight – and I've always enjoyed that: it's only human. No more signing autographs, which I was always pleased to do, except when grown-up fans tried to give you their views on life while you obliged. I recognised that autographs meant a lot to youngsters and never refused one, though I sometimes wished that the kids who flocked around the teams during the half-time break at Stradey would wait until the final whistle.

I knew that I would miss rugby's unique after-the-match atmosphere, when suddenly men stop being opponents hell-bent on thrashing each other and talk amicably over a pint of beer and a sandwich. (In my experience very few players broke this rule by transporting hostility from the field to the club-house.) And, I reflected, I would miss the coaches, certainly the major influence upon the game in my time.

My first impulse when asked for an opinion on coaching used to be to reply, 'Coaches and coaching never influence the way I play the game.' But long thought has convinced me that I was wrong. First I see that I fitted easily into the modern game as it is played in Britain. Nowadays, for example, you can join any XV in Wales, from the national XV to a scratch charity team, and straight away feel like a square peg in a square hole. Under the Irish coach Syd Millar in South Africa I was never asked to modify my style one iota. So I conclude that the basic aims and intentions of the coaches rubbed off upon me without my consciously realising it.

I applaud the coaching system, chiefly because it demands that someone views the play objectively with ample opportunity to see what may be going wrong and why. In the old days captains were required to undertake the analytic role, and because of their close involvement in the action it was an impossible task. Good coaches, too, can foster a team approach, not just in training or in a pre-match talk but also at meal-times and on social occasions.

The criticism levelled against them is that they smother the flair and genius of individual players in their enthusiasm for team-work. That may be true of bad coaches, but the good ones recognise that in a level-pegging situation, with two teams pitted against each other who have been coached to the nth degree, it is up to the gifted individual to make a break-through and crack the stale-mate. Good coaches hammer home the basics, but never dogmatically: there is always flexibility in their make-up.

I was lucky enough to play under four great coaches. The first was John Dawes, and sometimes it feels as if this delightful, puckish character has been breathing down my neck ever since I first met him on joining London Welsh in 1968. Besides being club coach he was the captain and had already been capped eleven times by Wales in the centre. Frankly, though, I didn't rate 'Sid' at first, considering him cumbersome and, to be blunt, fat! He made few breaks and as far as I could see possessed no side-step or swerve. It was only gradually that it dawned on me what a subtle, genuinely clever player he was, a beautiful timer of a pass who never delivered bad ball to his co-centre or wing.

John and I played many games together for London Welsh and Wales after that time, and following my own move back to Swansea he succeeded Clive Rowlands as Wales team coach so that our regular contact was revived and extended. And all the time my respect for him grew. He has an ice-cold brain, which is forever searching for and identifying opportunities for using possession fruitfully, for instance by counter-attack off one's own try-line to take the opposition by surprise. His inventiveness is applied to training sessions, which always contain some new gimmick or other and never become dull. He never bawls anyone out: at most, if you make a mistake, he calls out 'donkey!' and fixes a wide-eyed stare upon you as if puzzled that anyone could be so stupid. He is a well-liked man, a character who makes people play for him, and that's a quality a coach needs to have.

I have never – and I mean never – known Dawes at a loss in seven years of big rugby. In defeat, a rare happening, he is philosophical: after our disappointing reverse at Murrayfield in 1975 he contented himself in the changing-room afterwards by saying, 'Hard luck, boys.' Only in the next squad session, ten days later, did he release blunt, pointed criticisms: 'The Scots won through our mistakes – some of you three-quarters dropped too many passes. We're going to cut those mistakes out.' That was all, but Ray Gravell, Steve Fenwick, John J. Williams and Gerald Davies worked like demons for the next hour to do what the man had said.

Dawes's commitment to coaching has been total, and the greatest compliment to him is that Llanelli, London Welsh, Wales and other sides who try to play attractive, imaginative rugby have followed his principles without demur. I think he will go a long way in rugby administration if he wants to, for he can be a superb diplomat. One caution: he does not always suffer fools gladly and in argument can bite the head off someone that he considers ill-informed.

John knows only two words of Welsh, *dim parcio* (no parking), which he once read outside a doctor's surgery and with which it gives him great amusement to accost his Welsh-speaking friends. One of them is Carwyn James, whose reputation as a coach is if anything higher than his own. Carwyn it was who coached the British Isles to their first-ever victorious overseas Test series this century in 1971, and then, as if to rub in the hoodoo he exercised over New Zealand sides, inspired his club, Llanelli, to their great win over the 1973 All Blacks.

Although I have spent a lot of time in Carwyn's company since our first proper meeting when the Lions assembled at Eastbourne in 1971 I don't think I can claim to know him even today. Dawes is one of the boys and fires out constant opinions on every subject under the sun; Carwyn always preserved a degree of aloofness and was often quiet and withdrawn. He doesn't appear to enjoy small talk, perhaps because his brain never stops ticking over.

As a coach I shall remember Carwyn for three qualities. First, his judgment: he knew just the kind of tour party that was needed for 1971. All of us were men who thirsted for victory, after being on too many losing sides against the All Blacks, and the coach both shared and fuelled our resolution. Secondly Carwyn went to great lengths to understand his men in order to extract the best from each of them: he appreciated that you could not motivate Gareth Edwards as you would Bob Hiller and that Barry John's genius differed from that of Mike Gibson. The third point is that Carwyn was a good listener: the Irish prop Ray McLoughlin knew the front-row game from A to Z, and the coach was a big enough man to soak up Ray's ideas on how to out-scrummage New Zealand and put them to profitable use.

Syd Millar, who coached the 1974 Lions, needed no such advice, since he had toiled for a dozen years in Ireland's front row and had been a British Isles prop in South Africa six years before. His earlier experience there made him an ideal choice, for he already knew about the pitfalls lying in store for unwary tourists, such as the perils of grass burns and the difficulties of playing at altitude on the high veld. He augmented this insight with a network of a hundred spies — Millar's Fifth Column! — who helped him to understand each successive team we met and dissect its strengths and weaknesses. He must be the best-informed coach I have ever worked with.

Syd aimed for one-hundred-per-cent forward dominance on that tour, and thanks to the presence in our ranks of hard, uncompromising performers like McBride, Carmichael, Brown, Uttley, Windsor and Mighty Mouse McLauchlan he achieved it. I am not too sure how flexible he would have shown himself and what alternative strategy he would have devised if South African packs had surpassed us, but that is a hypothetical question since the need never arose. In training periods Millar spent most of his time with the forwards and was fortunate to be able to leave the backs' manoeuvres in the hands of J. P. R. Williams, Ian McGeechan and Mike Gibson when he arrived. My only criticism of his coaching was that it lacked variety, and we all tended to become bored in the last stages of a hard afternoon's work.

All three of these coaches favoured a cool approach, with little raising of the voice. I believe they realised that on the whole their charges were intelligent men who all had points of view and something to contribute. I suspect that the modern generation of rugby players thinks harder and more earnestly than its predecessors, and certainly today's Lions and International men respond best to quiet, constructive criticism. Loud-mouthed scoldings or histrionics leave them cold.

Mention of histrionics brings me to Clive 'Top Cat' Rowlands, Wales's team coach between 1968 and 1974. Although towards the end of his reign senior Internationals found them repetitive and somewhat overdone, I have to admit that Clive's team-talks immediately before a big game were superb performances and had to be heard to be believed. Every ounce of *hwyl*, that Welsh mixture of excitement and bravado, was injected into the atmosphere. The coach would stalk the room, jabbing a finger there, pounding a fist here, as he raised our morale to fever-pitch. 'You're going to win for Wales,' he would declaim, 'for your fathers, your mothers, your wives, your girl-friends, your children, even for your Aunty Gwladys.' The boys would nod eagerly, flex their muscles, breathe in deeply through flared nostrils, and stride off towards the arena ready to scatter the foe to the four winds. Only once did a close back-row colleague of mine stop as he was about to trot on to the Cardiff Arms Park turf and say with a puzzled frown, 'Hey, wait a minute — I haven't got an Aunty Gwladys.'

Even though I consider that at the outset Clive's rugby knowledge was not as profound as that of, say, John Dawes, he learned speedily enough and was undoubtedly the best motivator I have known. As one of the first-ever national team coaches in the British Isles he was treading largely unknown territory and had to work out a mode of operation from scratch. I expect he would be the first to acknowledge the debt he owes to Ray Williams, of whom more in a later chapter; but the creation of team-spirit was all his own work, and when we members of his Grand Slam side of 1971 used to say that we would die for each other, we really meant it!

Yes, I concluded, the coaches had been the midwives to British rugby's renaissance, a major influence for good in my time. I anticipated that sooner or later there would be pressure on me to join their number — but that was something that could wait. One decision was enough on a sunlit, rather drug-happy morning in a hospital ward: Merv the Swerve would hang up his boots.

2 *Overture and Beginnings*

David Parry-Jones

One of the sorriest sporting scapegoats of all time must be the Newport back-row forward John Jeffrey, who was tossed at the age of nineteen into the bubbling cauldron of Wales's 1967 clash with New Zealand. His team found themselves trailing 8-3 soon after half-time but were busily playing their way back into contention when the All Blacks stormed forward in pursuit of a penalty attempt which dropped short of the posts. Jeffrey clutched the ball, fumbled it, and in a panic jerked away a careless pass on to which Davis pounced to score what turned out to be a decisive try. Others have got away with more heinous crimes, but the youngster's harsh penalty was to play ten more years of first-class rugby without ever sniffing a Welsh team place again.

In retrospect Jeffrey's clanger can be seen to have cleared the stage for Mervyn Davies's entry upon the International scene some fifteen months later. Wales were searching for a number 8 forward to succeed Alun Pask, and besides discarding Jeffrey they experimented unsuccessfully with Dennis Hughes of Newbridge; Ron Jones, a big tough exile from the ranks of Coventry; Wanbon, an Aberavon forward who cashed his chips and went North immediately after scoring an important try against England at Twickenham; and Gallacher of Llanelli, in trials. Neath's Dai Morris was another guinea-pig, but after a couple of appearances at number eight he won his next thirty-two caps as a flanker. All these men possessed great qualities without quite approaching the all-round skills in tight and open play which Pask had demonstrated for the previous seven seasons.

Although as raw as Jeffrey on his first appearance, Mervyn

Davies, as we shall see, was the first of the bunch properly to seize his chance and embark upon a remarkably long-lived career. It is idle to speculate, but had the Newport player not slipped up in that first outing, Merv the Swerve might have been the man condemned to sit on the side-lines, so that a decade later it seems as if chance had a hand in his long reign in the middle of Wales's back row. Yet there is a moral to the story, which is that in the bad old days forwards commonly bore the brunt of criticism for a major reverse, and many more of their number are revealed in the record-books as 'one-cap wonders'. On the other hand, if scrum halves or stand-offs had a bad day it was because they 'lacked protection' or received 'bad ball'. The critics would explain that the real trouble lay up front, where the props were buckling, the locks not shoving or the back row breaking too soon.

For the game on the field used to be a two-tier society. In cricket there are fast bowlers, or cavalier batsmen, and the rest. Heavyweights and strikers are the men the crowds flock to see, rather than flyweights and stopper centre-halves. Equally, rugby was divided into 'them' and 'us'. The backs were an aristocracy, who expected as a right to be supplied with regular possession in order to demonstrate moves which, it was implied, were beyond the wit of the average forward to understand, let alone take part in. Forwards lacked the capacity to do more than one thing at a time: they could think, or handle or run; but they ought not to attempt a combination of any two of these. They were allowed to 'support' moves, but on the whole were encouraged to think of themselves as a humble service industry.

And in popular esteem it has to be admitted that down the years right to the present day, backs, like goal-scorers and 15-stone boxers, have drawn the biggest response from the ranks of enthusiasts. For they are the men most likely to alter the course of a match suddenly and dramatically. When the ball reaches the hands of a Gerald Davies, a David Duckham or an Andy Irvine — then the crowd expects something to happen. They are the consummators, and in rugby lore it is they who become heroes. Forwards find it hard to be awarded residence in Valhalla unless they happen to have been leaders, like Watcyn Thomas, the austere John Gwilliam or

England's Eric Evans and Wavell Wakefield. Their cleverer tricks or accomplishments are remembered, like the high-altitude ability of Roy John in the fifties. So are their work-a-day virtues, such as Budge Rogers's industry, Hugh McLeod's consistency, or Bryn Meredith's ubiquity. But superlatives are reserved for backs, and even the tremendous combination of Marques and Curry, perhaps the best pair of locks British rugby has seen, is talked of rather as the farming community would assess a pair of loyal, dutiful oxen. Forwards have always been candidates for big, blue rosettes, not crowns of laurel.

It seems to me, however, that this traditional view has been changing. Certainly Merv the Swerve (the affectionate nick-name is a clue in itself) has been perhaps the first forward to radiate the kind of charisma which had hitherto emanated only from backs. The broad, white head-band was both a trade-mark and an eye-catching indication of his involvement in the action. Wherever he moved on the field eyes followed him, and he was seen to be dominant in the play as only half-backs had previously been. His skills were self-evident: full use of height plus accurate catching and steering down of the ball at lines-out; strength applied constructively at mauls; an inventive eagerness to vary tactics at the scrummage coupled with a willingness to take pressure off the inside-half; cross-field covering in what appeared to be seven-league boots and the ruthless cutting-down of midfield attackers in the act of piercing the defence — 'Don't worry,' the grand-stand aficionados would reassure each other, 'Merv's there!'

In one important respect Mervyn Davies was luckier than his predecessors: by early 1969, when he received his first cap against Scotland, Clive Rowlands was in command as coach and had embraced the idea of the 'squad' approach to competitive rugby. Its essence was coherence, its method the perfecting of drills, and it changed the status of forwards overnight: henceforth they would be constantly in touch with play, not as second-class citizens but as innovators and entrepreneurs.

Before this, the nearest thing to squads in Britain had been the first and second XV groups which practised together at schools and the universities. Oxford's Blue side, for example, was both opposed in training and covered for injury by the Greyhounds, and likewise Cambridge by the LX Club. It was this togetherness, with first-strings and reserves all playing an imaginative but fundamentally uniform game, which until a decade ago kept Oxbridge in the van of British rugby and on terms with bigger, stronger opponents. Many a Blue would experience acute disillusionment when he moved off to the club scene and discovered the lax, casual attitude to training, with senior members of the side chorusing, 'None of those fancy varsity tricks here, young man.' Now the universities' methods are no longer unique and disappointment is sometimes expressed at the declining standards of Oxbridge play. But it is not they who have gone back; rather, their system has been adopted and perfected by clubs and, most intensively, by national XVs.

Thus on entering the Welsh squad Mervyn Davies found that his role had been pre-cast for him, as had every detail of the co-operation to be expected between the back row trio of himself, Dai Morris and John Taylor, a London Welsh colleague. For the Londoners it was time-consuming to travel on Sundays to Port Talbot's seaside lido for training sessions or to Cardiff in mid-week for pre-International run-outs and team talks. But on such occasions their game was refined and polished, while thorny problems like back-row defence on one's own try-line were thrashed out and solved. The new forward felt that he was joining an outfit which expected a precise contribution from him, and this has been true of all recruits to the Welsh pack since 1969. It has become fashionable to speak of a Wales 'shadow XV'; that is, the reserve half of a thirty-strong squad, with each position covered by an heir apparent.

So Mervyn Davies was a product of modern collective methods, on to which he grafted considerable individual skills and purpose. There is one other point to make: his career was characterised by the coolest imaginable approach. His game could not have been harder or more robust but he was always a model of decorum, an example you could happily commend to a small son. In the most demanding circumstances he was never guilty of a mean or underhand action, seldom of a show of temper or temperament. These are the kind of reasons why he received four thousand letters in hospital, and made him someone special — an aristocrat among forwards.

MERVYN DAVIES

I came of age in rugby football during 1969, and since it all happened in rather sensational fashion the details are engraved on my mind as if it were yesterday.

In January of that year, after a bare three months in the first-class game, I had travelled to Cardiff in response to an emergency summons to play at number 8 in the WRU's final trial, stepping into the place of Newbridge's Dennis Hughes, who had withdrawn from the Probables team because of a leg injury. Although we won comfortably, I had subsequently put the idea of selection for the national XV right out of my mind, for I assumed that Dennis would be fit to claim his place at Murrayfield in the first match of our International campaign against Scotland. So here I was the following Friday, driving to morning school back in Surrey and halting outside a Guildford newsagent for my friend and teaching colleague Chris Morgan to pick up a newspaper.

When he emerged he was waving it in the air and seemingly speechless. Finally he managed to gasp hoarsely, 'Merv, you're in – you're IN!' I seized the paper from him and, sure enough, tucked away low on the back page (for popular London newspapers don't give much prominence to rugby, especially Welsh rugby) was my name among the XV listed by Wales for the Murrayfield match.

We looked at each other, wide-eyed. Chris clasped my hand. Then we began to whoop our delight – and straight away decided that school would have to do without us that day. I am afraid that the pair of us played truant and spent a large part of the ensuing hours in a hostelry called The Seven Stars, which was sadly blasted by the IRA some years later.

That evening I would go up to the London Welsh HQ at Richmond to pick up congratulatory telegrams and enjoy the pats on the back. But first I rang home and spoke to my mother, who was beside herself with joy. It was disappointing not to be able to talk with my father, who had left for work – he had wanted to contact me the previous evening, when the news was known in Wales, but my flat-mates and I were not on the telephone. However, I well knew how thrilled he would be, and I reflected how sensible had been his influence upon my sporting career. As one who had represented Wales in the so-called 'Victory' Internationals, he must have been keen for me to play and excel at rugby, yet he had never pressed the game on me.

Thus as a small boy I had been quite happy kicking a soccer-ball around the parks and playgrounds of suburban Swansea. Even when I moved on to my secondary school, Penlan, where they introduced me to rugby, I still enjoyed out-of-school soccer matches, in which, because of my height, I liked to play centre-forward. Mention of positions prompts me to record my view that the position chosen for a youngster by his rugby coach at school is crucially important for the later development of his career. I have one close friend who, in my opinion, might have become an International scrum-half, but since he was made into a flanker at school, a flanker he remained, even though in the senior game he was manifestly too small for the position. So I would urge all schoolmasters constantly to reassess the capabilities of the pupils under their care and not to decide, 'Once a prop, always a prop,' and so on. I know that they have to produce good school XVs but they also have a duty to help boys to realise their best potential.

Fortunately my size and weight dictated my position, and at fourteen, after a season on the wing, I was switched by the rugby master Gwyn Waters to number 8, which was to be my berth for the next fifteen years. Other sports held appeal, especially athletics, in which I was a long-jumper, and basketball, which I commend to all youngsters wanting to improve their agility and handling skills; but it was during the winter and the rugby season that I found I could best satisfy my appetite for physical exertion. The contact element in the game stirred me, and I took pleasure in tackling and putting a man down hard so that he would be less of a threat in the succeeding action.

In the sixth form I became the school vice-captain of rugby and had a Welsh Secondary Schools trial or two without catching the selectors' eyes. To be honest I didn't very much enjoy these occasions, for as my school's sole representative I found myself travelling to and from trials on my own, and I think companionship is all-important in rugby. I re-experienced that feeling of being an outsider when, as a Swansea Training College student, I took part in trials for the Welsh Colleges XV. Once more it was fashionable establishments like the Caerleon and Cardiff training colleges whose candidates found favour, and men like Roger Lane and John Jeffrey kept me out of the reckoning. Later on, of course, the tables were to be turned.

I cannot say that I actively looked forward to teaching as a career, but by mid-1968 I had been unable to think of anything I preferred. Teaching seemed to offer a secure future and there were plenty of jobs available; so along with a crowd of my Swansea fellow students who decided that it would be pleasant to stick together I applied for a post in Surrey. Five of us were taken on, and we moved *en bloc* to Guildford in September and jointly rented a flat.

I realised that no quick riches would be coming my way, for my first month's salary amounted to just £52, but it allowed for the inner man's needs to be catered for and was enough for me to buy my first car – a Mini, into which I daily squeezed my large frame to drive to the Mitchett Junior School. Here, though I had been trained to teach physical education, my duties turned out to be fairly general and I took several subjects.

It was in the Mini that, before long, I set out one evening up the A3 (a journey I grew to hate because of the heavy rush-hour traffic) to take part in a London Welsh training session. I had turned out once or twice for that agreeable club, the Old Guildfordians, only to find that their rugby was less demanding and interesting than I had hoped, so I became determined to make the move to something better. The London Welsh club seemed an obvious choice, and to help convince them that I might be a useful back-row recruit I presented a letter from Swansea, for whom I had been chosen a couple of times while at college, and had acquitted myself reasonably well in a Christmas fixture against Watsonians.

The welcome at Old Deer Park was at once warm and generous, and although I had to start in the third XV (for whom I scored three tries on my debut) I was at once made to feel a true club member. There were numerous young teachers on the strength, and senior stalwarts who knew the size of our incomes made sure we were never short of a pint and some good company after training. My first changing-room was, I recall, the hockey team's hut, for facilities at the club in those days were not as palatial as they are to-day. Once out on the pitch, though, I knew that I was on the edge of the big time, for the giants were at hand: Dawes himself, Tony Gray, Geoff Evans, Bill Hullin, and of course John Taylor, who struck me as a bit gruff and distant at first. I soon became impressed with the London Welsh's operational slickness, whereby a com-mittee man kept a close eye on the talent available at each level within the club, so that the right candidate could be promoted on merit or to replace an injured player in the premier sides.

A former Welsh trialist, Colin Bosley, supervised the second XV, and it was on his recommendation that I got my own promotion. I had gone down to Swansea for my first half-term holiday to tell the folks how their school-master son was getting on, when a card arriv-ed from Old Deer Park asking me to report back on the Saturday to play for the first XV against Moseley. Tony Gray, capped by Wales the previous spring, had damaged a shoulder, so Mervyn Davies's services were required. My parents were so pleased that they decided to return to Surrey with me, stayed the night at our flat and were spectators at the ground in the afternoon. They saw a London Welsh victory by 14 points to 5.

It's hard to be dropped from a successful side, so after that good start on 2 November I retained my place throughout the month. Even when Tony came back, I continued to be picked at number 8 with Gray and Taylor as flankers, and we laid the foundations of a well-balanced back-row partnership that was to last several seasons. John was an excellent handler and distributor of the ball; Tony was the speed-merchant who got to the break-down first; while I grafted away as a ball-winner in all situations. This suited me, for I had no desire to earn the reputation of a whizz-kid, always haring around the park and joining in glamour moves!

The first-class game seemed to hold few terrors for me, and I consider that I made the transition into the higher echelon smoothly. Only once did I feel a bit rueful in those early weeks: we were busi-ly administering a London Welsh-type thrashing to Newport, then Welsh champions, when one of the Black and Ambers' back-row players, George Patterson, knocked out one of my front teeth. It was an accident, I feel sure, but it dented my pride and, for a day or two, my zest for the game! However, I became established in the London Welsh first XV, and began my rapid conversion to their thoughtful, imaginative way of playing the game.

I was aware that one of our committee, Harry Bowcott, was a member of Wales's 'Big Five' selectors and kept his fellows in touch with rising talent at Old Deer Park. But I was still stunned when, following the club's Christmas tour in South Wales, the call came to my country's final trial at Cardiff Arms Park – this after a mere twenty first-class games. For at that juncture in my career I had formed no ambition at all to move into representative contention: I simply wanted to enjoy my rugby and improve my own perform- ance by watching and listening to men like Dawes and Taylor. So when I reported to the Cardiff changing-room I was still rather daz- ed by my progress. Everything had happened so easily, it seemed. Three months before my team-mates had been the Old Guildford- ians; now here I was pulling on a red jersey next to players like 'Ben' Price, of Newport, Denzil Williams, Gareth Edwards and Gerald Davies. For once, though, I didn't feel a loner, since fellow London Welshmen like Dawes and Taylor were present, as was John P. R. Williams who, after his Argentine tour with Wales, was now bidding for a first full cap.

Clive Rowlands helped to settle us all down by emphasising before the kick-off that the selectors would not be choosing on in- dividual brilliance but were anxious to see how each of us could fit into team play. I felt relief, since at that time I much preferred to slot myself into a plan dictated by others, and told myself, 'This is just another match – I'll go out and play my normal game' – with one difference: I knew how John Jeffrey had been dropped after one mistake as Wales's number 8, and I was determined that there should be no errors made by me that day. I recall very little of the occasion, except that we won 24-3 and a new back-row colleague Dai Morris snapped up three tries. And to emphasise my rawness, when the then selector, Rees Stephens, patted me on the back afterwards and said, 'Well played, son,' I looked at him blankly and said, 'Thanks, but who are you?'

However, it seemed that I had done enough. Without waiting for Dennis Hughes to prove his fitness the selectors made up their minds, and seven mornings later, the day after we saw the news of my first cap outside the Guildford newsagent's shop, through the letter-box of the flat came tumbling the magic invitation: 'You have been selected to play for Wales against Scotland next Saturday 7 February. Please delete as necessary and return this card within five days.' Then it added, 'I can/cannot play.' I crossed out the last word but one, borrowed a stamp, resealed the card in its envelope and had it back in a pillar-box all within sixty seconds of opening it up! You don't need five days to decide on accepting a first cap!

I recall that pre-match arrangements were spelled out by the Welsh Rugby Union with great clarity, so that no newcomer could be uncertain what his movements were to be during the week-end. The directive stated that we would be required to train at the Bridgend police ground on the following Thursday, and detailed our move to a Cardiff hotel as well as the full schedule between our flight from Rhoose airport and our return there from Edinburgh on the Sunday morning. The WRU appeared to be quite well organised, and in my mind were sown the seeds of a respect for our administrators which has survived down the years.

That is not to say that I have been uncritical of them. My contemporaries and I have had to coax them to move with the times and bring their thinking up to date, so helping to make other nations envious of the way the game is run in Wales. For instance the first time I played in a home International, against Ireland at Cardiff in 1969, my ration of tickets amounted to one free stand seat only, with an option to buy a second. By the time I played my thirty-eighth game, in March 1976, an International player could receive two complimentary stand tickets, and had in addition the right to buy two more as well as eight for the enclosure and four for the field. I think that is reasonably fair, but it has taken some argument and persuasion.

This has also been the case with the social niceties. In 1969 a wife who wanted to be with her husband the night after an International game might have to sneak into a hotel and kip down next to her burly spouse in a single bed! Women's lib — or even married couples' lib – had not penetrated the WRU. Now wives and fiancées are accommodated and entertained by the WRU, so that their menfolk can take the field without wondering anxiously if they have a seat or even a view of the match, and how they will amuse themselves that evening. This is civilised, and it is appreciated by all concerned. Mind you, I have not always been in favour of women being present at big rugby games: at the first International game I ever saw I was accompanied on to Cardiff's east terrace by two short teenage girl friends who couldn't see over the heads of the people in front. They kept demanding to be hoisted aloft, and I endured aching shoulders and biceps for days as a result!

My contemporaries and I were also perfectly happy at the accommodation provided for us. The WRU always chose the best hotels in Edinburgh and Dublin, and perfectly adequate places in London and Paris where costs are somewhat higher. Nor was there any limit to what you could have to eat: if a 16-stone lock wanted two steaks for dinner then he simply ordered them. Perhaps, though, there may be room for a more generous and flexible approach to the paying of players' travelling expenses by road and train. International players do not seek to make money out of appearing for Wales – many of us, I know, would almost be prepared to pay for the privilege! But, seriously, I do believe that at such a level men have an absolute right not to be out of pocket.

What, you may well ask, should the authorities expect in return for being realistic and even generous in their treatment of players? As far as I am concerned, and I am sure this goes for all my contemporaries, the very best behaviour one is capable of. On trains, in the street, at hotels, in airport lounges, on duty, at leisure, I always bore in mind that I was carrying the flag for my country. Players know very well that a bad-tempered word to a supporter, a frown instead of a smile, reflects not just on them but also on the game in the principality and on Wales itself. They are not just eighty-minute ambassadors for their country.

Having said all that I must add that as far as I can tell the Welsh top brass are more enlightened than the other home unions. For a start they are always approachable as human beings, whereas my English friends tell me that their administrators sometimes stand on their dignity and become aloof. The average Welsh selector in my time has been a decent bloke, the kind to whom you could pour out your troubles over a quiet drink if you were a new, young member of the Welsh squad in need of reassurance. It helps, too, when young men like Keith Rowlands join the Big Five, for their generation is more in touch with the needs and the desires of modern players.

Mention of the squad calls to mind the big controversy in Wales over whether our refined squad system renders international trial matches irrelevant and unnecessary. That is an argument I have heard advanced by leading critics, who say that the eighty minutes the probables spend playing the possibles is a waste of time and that we should be better employed having a teach-in with our coach. It is true that whereas once upon a time trial form was the all-important thing, in 1976 Elgan Rees of Neath could score four tries in our final trial and still know that he would not dislodge Gerald Davies or J. J. Williams from their positions as Wales's wingers. That must have been a chastening experience for him.

Yet trials do have their uses. Up-and-coming players can be chosen for a squad and know that they belong in the selectors' plans. But they still need to be tested and observed against seasoned performers under match conditions. There is also the point that it is through a good trial performance that a player often gains entry to the squad, which is the final stepping-stone to a cap. And once a man is in the squad, then the sitting tenant has to look to his laurels. I used to be very wary of the challenge from year to year of men like Dennis Hughes, John Jeffrey and my big pal Derek Quinnell, and would redouble my efforts to maintain peak form. Hefin Jenkins of Llanelli is another squad member whom I have learned to respect: a brilliant handler and runner with the ball, but one whose game has so far lacked the consistency necessary to win caps.

England, of course, need trials because their playing strength is so scattered. A man from Penzance might be picked to lock with a Northumbrian, and such fixtures are a means of uniting them and dove-tailing their abilities. However, England overdo it. In the autumn of 1975 their long, tortuous trials system was, I believe, the reason why they did not get the best out of Mark Keyworth, the

Shropshire lad who plays for my own club, Swansea. The English selectors called on him to play trials on four successive Saturdays, a fortnight after which he got his first cap. But I am sure that the strain of playing five major games in six weeks took a toll of his energy which his national selectors did not appreciate. Nor did it seem fair to Swansea that we were robbed of his contribution for six Saturdays on the trot, for of course we gave him the customary match off a week before his first appearance for England.

However, back to 1969 and the exciting journey towards my first cap. That trip to Scotland with the Welsh team was my first flight, a forerunner of scores I have made since, though not in quite so strung-up a condition, for a young man on the eve of playing for his country for the first time has a wonderful sense of being about to step into history.

Since I have already digressed more than a little, let us end this chapter with a few other reflections on occasions when I have been airborne in the company of a crowd of rugby men. My own way of passing the time was to read a good book and, as a fairly cool customer, the only time I have ever been seriously alarmed for our safety was during a flight through the mountains of New Zealand's South Island in 1971. That was a trip when Ireland's sturdy prop Sean Lynch had to be literally held down in his seat by his countryman Willie John McBride after observing that we were actually flying below the towering, snow-capped peaks on each side of our eight-seater plane! Carwyn James, in contrast, preserved a tight-lipped silence, and even I had a strange feeling in the pit of my stomach as we passed over knife-edged ranges and suddenly found ourselves gazing down into awesome crevasses below.

In fact quite a number of players who are hard as nails on the field have a horror of flying, and I fear that on tour they have the mickey cruelly extracted from them by the rest. On embarkation, for instance, good fliers among the Lions would immediately give throat to a mournful rendition of the popular song, 'This could be the last time'! Those with no nerves would also gather, especially at the end of a tour, in the stewardesses' bar at the rear of the aircraft in an attempt to drink it dry before landing at Heathrow; once, on the way back from the Far East, an ashen-faced member of the apprehensive brigade tip-toed down to us and implored, 'Please, you lot, come back to your seats — the captain's just said on the tannoy that we have too much weight in the tail and are losing height rapidly.' A captain, I suspect, with a sense of humour.

Some of the best flying yarns concern Pontypool's ace hooker, the British Lion Bobby Windsor. The 'Duke' flew only under protest, and when a seagull winged its way into one of our engines shortly after our take-off from a South African airport in 1974, causing us to circle and land again, he left the plane smartly with the curt information that he would be making the journey to our next fixture by road — all three hundred miles of it! On another occasion the Wales XV were bound for North America on a jumbo jet belonging to Air Canada, which is a bilingual airline with two official languages, English and French. The Duke clamped ear-phones over his head and with an expression that slowly became more and more fixed settled down to watch the in-flight film. After half-an-hour's extreme concentration he turned round and said, 'I don't know why I'm watching this film — I can't understand a word of it.' We pointed out that if he switched his control knob from French to English he might gain more insight into the plot!

Air travel is usually long-drawn-out and boring, but it certainly makes the world smaller for the rugby jet-set of today. And when I remember my early journeys by Mini up the A3 to Old Deer Park, even a transcontinental flight to Tokyo seems bearable by contrast.

3 *With Wales in Europe*

David Parry-Jones

Standing ovations for popular figures on their retirement or after some great achievement are not uncommon, especially when the liquor or a tide of emotion, or both, are running strongly. But when the same person is accorded two such ovations, each two minutes in duration, during the same function, then clearly the beneficiary is no ordinary man.

It happened in June 1976 at the annual dinner which Welsh Brewers throw at the Bindles Ballroom, Barry, for the champion club and Challenge Cup winners in the Welsh domestic season. By now it has become the premier summer occasion of the rugby calendar, with invitations treasured as if they were International tickets. The buses, limousines and television vans bear down on the agreeable sea-front restaurant carrying all manner of folk from peers of the realm to face-workers freshly showered after eight hours underground. There are mayors, ministers of religion and masseurs, club presidents, professors and policemen, cartoonists, comedians and record cap-holders, and adolescents with down on their cheeks not long out of the junior ranks.

And this night the tall figure of Mervyn Davies was making a first public appearance since the crisis. A little against his will, for he still tired easily, he had been irresistibly drawn by the desire to greet old friends and opponents and through a sense of obligation to the special nature of the celebration, which would also be in honour of his Grand Slam XV. At the reception he moved happily among fellow guests, his evident stiffness emphasising the slight stoop born of hours spent conversing with shorter men than he, before tucking into his meal at a table shared with congenial companions like

c

Gerald Davies and Gareth Edwards.

The first accolade came when the president and host for the evening, Dennis Urquhart, formally welcomed him to the banquet and expressed the community's relief at his return to health. As one man the room rose and applauded while Merv, a little overcome, waved a large paw in acknowledgment. A repeat performance took place at the climax to the evening when, to the raucous strains of 'For he's a jolly good fellow', the captain came forward to accept his award — for the second Year running — as Wales's Player of the Year, elected by the Welsh Rugby Writers' Association. On the advice of his doctors he left for Pontlliw well before midnight and eschewed the carousing which would continue into the early hours of the morning; but it had still been a night to remember.

Although the warmth of his reception owed a lot to genuine pleasure and gladness at his recovery (the now bristling crew-cut was a clear reminder of the ordeal he had been through) another consideration prolonged and intensified the hand-clapping. From the outset of his career Mervyn Davies had been a success symbol, who stood for winning rugby; and the Welsh, not a nation noted for world-conquering achievements in other spheres, set much store by victory in the handling game. We ought not to be hypocritical about this, for though we have a healthy appetite for open, spectacular rugby, when the past is recalled and record books thumbed through, it is not the quality of a particular match that comes to mind, but who won it. Whatever protestations Welsh fans may make publicly, it is my belief that when the stakes are at their highest, as in a contest involving their age-old rivals New Zealand, for example, they would prefer victory in a poor game by 3-0 to defeat by 24-20 in a great match.

Be that as it may, Mervyn Davies's record in terms of success is certainly remarkable. Its highlights and longevity also characterise the careers of a select few others like Gareth Edwards, Gerald Davies and J. P. R. Williams; but while they are likely to be seen in retrospect as adornments to the game, superb artists in their own right but essentially individualists and solo turns, Merv will surely be viewed as a lynch-pin, a grafter supreme who created conditions under which the backs' genius could flower and run up points.

Moreover he finally assumed the captaincy of his country and demonstrated that he could transmit his own earnest desire for supremacy and his methods of achieving it to fourteen colleagues.

Take the statistics. His career closed with eight wins in nine outings as Wales's skipper, the odd game out being a reverse at Murrayfield when his side's rhythm was disturbed by two injuries necessitating replacements during the match. He will argue that coaching had sown the seeds of success, but the fact is that for eighty minutes in each game the decisions were his. The depth of his concentration was revealed by the attention paid to details like which place-kickers to employ of the three under his command: Bennett, Steve Fenwick and Alan Martin were all used at the right time.

He played thirty-eight times for his country, overhauling Denzil Williams's record as the most-capped forward at Dublin in 1976, and was on losing sides only eight times. There were twenty-six victories in his time, during the whole of which Wales ran up 657 points and conceded 379 (and these are figures which do not include the heavy scoring against newer rugby nations like Canada and Japan). For the British Isles he appeared in two triumphant Test series, during which five games were won, two drawn and one lost. Thus in forty-six appearances against the most formidable opposition he tasted defeat a mere nine times. In comparison the copy-books of Gerald Davies and Gareth Edwards are slightly blotted by their presence on the unsuccessful South African tour of 1968, so that only J. P. R. Williams could match his former captain's winning percentage.

As Mervyn's career matured, the records also disclose how effectively his defensive skills eventually eliminated scoring opportunities for back-row and half-back opponents close to the scrum. The last number 8 forward to score against him was Ripley at Twickenham in 1974 (when the video-tape shows an Englishman to have been accidentally offside); and in earlier years Kirkpatrick, Lochore, Ian Robertson, Goodall, Hannaford, Dauga and Colin Telfer all found ways of eluding his clutches. But from summer 1974, the path to the try-line was effectively barred to attackers who came within his sphere of influence — in his last thirteen representative matches only eight tries at all were scored against the Lions or Wales.

To balance the books it ought to be conceded that he was not noted for try-scoring himself. He never scored for the Lions in Tests and got only two tries for Wales, both against England at Twickenham. Nobody who saw it, though, could forget the try which earned a draw for the Barbarians on the same ground against the All Blacks in 1974: Irvine had made it possible, but the Welshman still needed the strength to break two tackles after backing up for a full 65 yards.

So for most of his representative career, Mervyn Davies was associated with victory, achieved and celebrated for the most part with a discernible nobility and magnanimity. He was never a glamour-boy, from whose toothpaste smile tripped silver words and honeyed sentiments – during television and radio interviews before as well as in his years as captain, there would be a furrowed brow and a painful gestation period before he gritted out short, terse answers to questions. But he brought home the bacon, and when he got his double ovation in 1976 it was largely because, as some ruefully realistic runner-up remarked at the Olympic Games that year, it's gold medals that count.

He began collecting them in 1969.

MERVYN DAVIES

I had a bad attack of nerves on the eve of my first appearance for Wales. To understand why, you have to imagine the pressure I felt under, which in turn was mainly the result of a progression to the Welsh XV that most people considered meteoric. I could sense that the fans were saying to themselves, 'In Wales we've scarcely heard of this raw number 8 from London Welsh – he can't be up to much.' The top Press reporters upset me with their sceptical predictions (and for that reason I never subsequently read newspaper previews throughout my career) and clearly did not rate me. I had to keep reminding myself that the selectors must be right and that my country needed me.

But it certainly cost me a lot of sleep. The two Johns, Dawes and Taylor (with whom the Big Five had sensibly put me to share a room), knew how it felt, and engaged me and J. P. R. Williams, also about to win a first cap, in a game of crib that lasted until mid-night. We didn't play for money, which was just as well since Dawes emerged well on top, underlining his private view that he is a world authority on the game. However, when the cards were finally put away and I climbed into bed I found it terribly difficult to drop off. Had success come too easily to Mervyn Davies? Had I had enough experience at the top level? I was not used to huge crowds, so would my nerves turn to jelly in front of 72,000 people? In short, was I heading for a fall?

The questions were still buzzing inside my head when I awoke, but from that point on there was no time to worry and fret. Once breakfast in bed was over there was to be total absorption not in personal fears and anxieties but in a positive approach to the business in hand, that of defeating the Scots. And on that day in Edinburgh, 15 February 1969, I worked out for myself a routine which was to vary little down the years, of a kind which most International players try to observe before a big occasion.

I liked to eat breakfast at about ten — a good fry-up of sausages, bacon, eggs, fried bread, tomatoes and so on — so that by lunch-time I would need no more than a small portion of fish with a few chips or, like J. P. R., some toast and honey. Some players would eat a steak, but this seemed to me a bad idea, for it takes twelve to sixteen hours to digest and can lie very heavily on the stomach during a match. We ate lunch in our team-room, where there were always jugs of orange squash available and also beer which the management thoughtfully provided but which the boys always generously left for our committee men — not a drop was ever wasted!

Between breakfast and lunch, however, the Wales team coach traditionally delivered his final pep-talk before a game, to which I listened all those years ago with a mixture of awe and mounting ex-citement. I have described Clive Rowlands's approach, but the traffic was by no means one-way. Every so often he would bark out the question, 'What are we going to do?' and as one man we had to bellow in reply, 'WIN!' Sometimes the challenge was posed to an individual, who also had to roar back, 'WIN!' — except that when burly John Lloyd of Bridgend was in the side he was allowed, in view of his well-known appetite, to respond, 'EAT 'EM!' Described coldly, all this may strike you as a hilarious bit of overacting (and I suspect that 'King' Barry John found it funny at the time, deeming it the braying of the donkeys who played in the pack), but it never seemed that way at the time, such was our complete involvement in preparing for action and intensifying team-spirit.

I was also introduced during that first pep-session to Wales's method of ensuring cohesion and rhythm up front. At scrummages, where we were trying hard to improve our technique at the time, the put-in warning by the inside-half – 'Coming in . . . now!' – is crucial for a good shove and a clean strike by the hooker. We listened to Gareth Edwards repeating the formula countless times, so that on the field we should be able to 'feel' the moment he fed the scrum and exert a snap shove. Mid-morning was also the time when everyone checked that he knew the range of signals, and even the new full-back, J. P. R. Williams, found that he was required to recognise where in the line-out our wing would throw the ball.

Checking boots and kit was the way I spent the final half hour or so before the Welsh team left its hotel for Murrayfield. The big lift to my morale continued as we drove from the city centre between pavements thronged with red-bereted supporters waving scarves and rattles and giving us the thumbs-up sign, and with kilted Scotsmen cat-calling or pretending to ignore our bus. At first I sat quiet and rather tense, but long before the end of the journey I had been coaxed into joining choral renderings of our Welsh battle songs along with Gareth Edwards, John Taylor and Jeff Young. Raymond 'Chico' Hopkins of Maesteg, so often Gareth's understudy, had the job of leading our final chant as we drew in at the SRU headquarters: 'Give us a "W", give us an "A", give us an "L",' and so on, until we finished with a fearsome cry of 'WALES!' (Chico successfully performed this role for the 1971 Lions, except on one occasion when his spelling let him down and we concluded by shouting, 'LOINS!')

About an hour before the kick-off we strolled together on to the Murrayfield turf to test its firmness and to sniff the atmosphere of the ground. It was only three-quarters full by that time, but perhaps because the popular terrace has no cover it always seemed a gigantic stadium, and that day I felt like an ant creeping along its floor. The feeling was intensified when finally we ran out for the kick-off (to my relief, for you don't get a cap until you actually cross on to the playing area: I had wrapped myself in cotton wool for the whole of the previous week) and I experienced the Murrayfield roar, which may not be quite as deafening as Hampden's but contained sufficient decibels for a beginner like me. It really was a moving experience, and I remember being unable to sing the national anthem for the lump in my throat.

All through the match I followed John Taylor's advice and tried to play as closely as possible with him and Dai Morris, who were flanking me in the back row. I aimed to cut errors out of my game and fulfil the role for which I had been chosen – the winning of the ball at line-out and maul – and because I do not honestly recall the tries by Gareth, Barry and Maurice Richards which helped us to a 17-3 victory, I conclude that I must have been pulling my weight in the middle of the forward struggle. Jim Telfer, my opposite number, and Alastair McHarg were the Scots who stand out in my memory, and I think that the latter could have been an even greater player had he concentrated on a single position instead of behaving one moment like a centre in full flight and the next as a lock forward. I must admit, though, that when he was in an opposing pack it felt like playing against four back-row forwards.

At the after-the-match banquet we celebrated hard, especially since we did not have to return to Cardiff until the following morning, and during the evening I could not help comparing the regal treatment accorded to me and my contemporaries with that experienced by my father's generation three decades earlier. Air travel for us, plush hotels to stay in, feasting and revelry after a game; when Dai Davies played for Wales at Murrayfield he travelled overnight on the Swansea-to-Edinburgh sleeper, met his team-mates in the dressing-room, played the match, and just had time for a bite of supper before catching the sleeper home again. But I don't think my father begrudges for a moment the fact that times have changed – for the better!

I had two minor disappointments at Murrayfield. First, I was not given an actual cap. In those days WRU officials did not carry new caps for awarding at away games (that's another reform they have since put through) so mine came in the post a week later. Inevitably it was too small, and when I sat for the obligatory photograph as demanded by fond parents, a slit needed cutting at the rear so that it would fit! It now has pride of place among my other trophies on the sideboard at home, and when it catches my eye it still gives me a kick to see it there.

Second, although Welshmen get just the one cap, at least we are given a new jersey for each match; my Murrayfield opposite number was strangely reluctant to do the usual final-whistle swap, and I later discovered that Scottish Internationals who part with their jerseys during a season have to pay for the next one they need. That struck me as penny-pinching on the part of the SRU.

Within two minutes of the kick-off in my second International, against Ireland in Cardiff, Brian Price had laid out Noel Murphy with a ferocious, perfectly aimed upper-cut.

In no more dramatic way could the extra dimension of rugby football at International level have been brought home to me. One minute all had been smiles and toothy grins as the teams were introduced to the Prince of Wales. The next, my captain had totally lost his cool and in response, I suspect, to some surreptitious provocation, had stretched the Irish flanker flat on his back. Brian, or 'Ben' as we called him, was normally the most placid of blokes and had earned my respect and gratitude for the calm assurance with which he had welcomed me into his side and the confidence he had instilled into the newcomer. Now here he was behaving as if momentarily demented and finding himself fortunate not to be sent off by Mr McMahon, the referee. Although we came out on top in the end, the game continued to be a disagreeable, tempestuous affair, and when Ken Kennedy was laid prostrate by a couple of our forwards, Tom Kiernan threatened to lead his men prematurely from the field.

Rugby is by definition a rough game, and at International level it is doubly volatile. The participants are without exception highly strung and the smallest thing is liable to upset them. But I must also point out that the game at all levels is played by some men (very few, I emphasise) who believe punching, gouging, kicking and trampling are all part of the afternoon's sport. Selection committees and referees could be stricter, but it is hard to see how such players can be effectively barred, and I fear they have to be tolerated if not condoned. Personally I never needed to practise foul play on anyone; I have large, bony shoulders and elbows which could always be dug with maximum and perfectly legitimate impact into someone who had roused my ire. I learned, too, to control my impatience and in order to exact satisfying retribution I might wait as long as twenty minutes or more before choosing the most inviting moment. On the field Merv had a long memory.

There is not much I can recall about the Paris game of 1969 except the unique Colombes atmosphere with bugles and trumpets blaring throughout, but we held on for a draw and needed only to beat England in Cardiff to finish ahead of Ireland, whose own title hopes we had foiled earlier. On the day the backs fairly sparkled to give us a 30-9 win with Maurice Richards scoring four times on the wing.

So, astonishingly, in my first Five Nations campaign we had ended on top of the pile, and wore a Triple Crown too. I cannot say that I yet felt established in the team, but I had the satisfaction of knowing that my contribution had been substantial.

I have dwelt in some detail on that first season of mine, partly because it gave all of us such pleasure, especially those who had collected a dozen or so caps without previously tasting the ultimate in success, but also since it underlined for me the potential of the squad system. The 5 am starts for our Aberavon beach sessions (in the days before the M4 it took five hours to reach South Wales from London); the long hours pounding the shingle to build stamina; endless scrummaging upon wet sand to knit our shove — all these hardships seemed worth the trouble. For, although amateur players, we were busy cultivating a professional attitude, by which I simply mean that we were single-mindedly determined to squeeze the very best out of ourselves. To squad sessions I probably owed the harmony struck by myself, Taylor and Dai Morris, who as a back row played a record eighteen International games together. People thought we made a perfect trio with my tight play, John's skills in the open and Dai's amazing stamina, which kept him perpetually on the ball and earned him the nick-name 'Shadow'. I was sorry that Dai never became a Lion; on the other hand he never liked being out of Wales and I wouldn't rule out the possibility that he let the selectors know privately that he didn't fancy a long tour. Why else would they have omitted him?

I must pay tribute here to Ray Williams, appointed in 1967 as the WRU's coaching organiser and the man who conceived the 'system' as we now know it in Wales, squads and all. He's a native of Wrexham, and when I first met him his northern vowels prompted me to inquire what part of England he was from. But it took no time at all to discover that this thorough Welshman knew more about rugby than anyone I had ever met — I still say that eight years later. He is Wales's rugby master-mind. His vision led him to see that coaching could bring success to the national XV (it did), and that this in turn would be the trigger to fire new enthusiasm for the game throughout Wales, in little boys eager to copy Barry John during a mini-rugby frolic, in school-leavers trembling on the verge of senior level, and even in veterans whose playing days were over but who might still plough back much wisdom and know-how. His administrative powers are considerable and his technical understanding unsurpassed.

Occasionally Gareth Edwards and I would venture to argue with him about the best route through which to channel back scrummed ball (he favoured the fastest, we inclined towards that which would give a scrum-half the best protection), but usually when Ray opened his mouth we listened. He certainly helped me with advice on playing the number 8 game — and that was rather unusual, for unless a coach had personal experience of playing in the position I usually gave him a piece of my mind if he tried to tell me how to improve my play.

Nor is Ray just a talker; when he challenged me to an elbow-press trial of strength the so-and-so usually won. If he wished to demonstrate a point during a squad session he would have no hesitation in choosing a big fellow like Denzil Williams to match himself against. For a long time during his playing career he was the leading stand-off half in the Midlands area of England, where he worked, and I believe he once turned down a Welsh trial in order to turn out

for the East Midlands against the All Blacks. He undoubtedly practised what he now preaches.

Because of a somewhat unexpected defeat in Dublin (to which I
shall return in a later chapter) we had to share the title with France
in 1970. So I remember the season chiefly because of the first try I
scored for Wales, which was touched down in my first
Twickenham International. It was a close thing, for I recall ground-
ing the ball on the line rather than over it. The men at the tail of
England's line-out were unprepared for a long throw on their own
corner flag, a gap opened up and a clean catch with some support
from Dai Morris did the rest. A big, exciting moment.

Later, after trailing 13-3 we won a titanic struggle by 17-13. I
suspect that when Gareth Edwards was substituted by Chico
Hopkins twenty minutes from the end, England's back row of
Bucknall, Taylor and West relaxed a little — fatally as it turned out,
for Chico put John Williams in for our second try and scored the
third himself.

We always used to say, 'If we've got to lose, let it not be against
England,' which was a particularly important maxim for those of us
who were London Welshmen and had to live cheek-by-jowl with
the Saxons! Thankfully in my time we suffered only one defeat at
their hands. And I must say, I enjoyed visiting 'HQ', not just for
the rugby but also for those palatial dressing-rooms and the seven-
foot baths in which even a bloke like me can stretch out and have a
soak.

After the slight disappointment of 1970, however, came the truly
outstanding Grand Slam triumph for Wales under John Dawes.
After comfortable wins over England and Ireland only a supreme
effort took us over the last hurdle in Paris, where J. P. R. Williams,
Denzil Williams and Barry John had great games, the last named
not only scoring a fine try but also putting in a suicidally brave
tackle to stop Benoit Dauga from reaching our line. However, there
is no doubt which game stands out as the greatest of that season and
perhaps the most nerve-racking I have ever taken part in: the clash
with Scotland at Murrayfield.

Five minutes from time we were behind 18-14, and for the life of
me I could not work out why. It was a sickening thought that after

playing pretty well, and scoring three tries, we were about to go down to defeat. Furthermore I had conceded six of the penalty points through which Scotland's skipper, Peter Brown, was keeping his side in the game with that unlikely kicking action of his. In my bones I felt guilt, but also a sense of injustice.

All the world remembers how Gerald Davies streaked away just before it was too late on a beautiful curve that took him around Scotland's wing and full-back for our fourth try. But the cover kept him away from the posts, so that when John Taylor was asked to attempt the conversion he had to make his mark just three yards from touch. I knew that he was on the correct side of the field for his left foot in-swing but I still half-covered my eyes, unwilling to follow the flight of the ball. Then, even before the crowd roared, I saw him turning back towards us, his eyes blazing and his arms waving with excitement – he hadn't watched the ball either, for immediately he kicked it he knew he had done everything right. John had saved my blushes, but more importantly, in retrospect, that conversion was the one thing that clinched a Grand Slam, out of 320 minutes of rugby.

The following year we continued to score heavily and it was an anticlimax to be robbed of a possible Grand Slam repeat by the political decision not to visit Dublin. But, inevitably I suppose, since rugby achievement goes in cycles, touching troughs as well as peaks, Wales obtained relatively mediocre results in the two seasons 1973 and 1974. New Zealand, Scotland, France and England all beat us during this time, we played a couple of dull draws, and as far as my career is concerned it was the least satisfactory period.

I think there were valid reasons for this. Perhaps I was somewhat to blame myself, for the couple of dozen caps I now owned had probably made me rather blasé. Clive Rowlands was undoubtedly tired and drained of ideas after his whole-hearted commitment to our cause for six years and the fire in his belly had burned low. We had a succession of different captains. Barry John had retired from the key stand-off half position, where his successor Phil Bennett was under all kinds of pressure. The front five of our pack, for so long the sturdy providers of quality possession for the brilliant back divisions, bore an unsettled look and were the constant objects of selectorial experiments. Other nations had imitated our squad system and were wise to tactics which had been novel when we introduced them, like J. P. R. Williams's entry into the line. All in all the odds were stacked against our continuing ability to win consistently.

Wales were going through a transitional period. The man chosen as captain of his country in 1975 had a lot of hard labour in front of him.

4 Captain of Wales

David Parry-Jones

Great players produced by Wales can be counted in dozens; her great captains on the fingers of one hand. Unanimity about their claim to lead, achievement on the field of play, and the absence of subsequent controversy or recrimination – these are the clues to greatness in a skipper, and until 1976 they pointed in the direction of only two post-war Welsh captains, John Gwilliam and John Dawes (and even the former has his detractors, who say that the teams he led could have brought off Grand Slams no matter who was skipper). Bleddyn Williams and Clive Rowlands come close to being bracketed with them; but Williams's days as captain were few, albeit successful, and 'Top Cat' is unfortunately associated with a somewhat negative and characterless period in the Welsh game.

Where, then, stands Mervyn Davies? Some rugby followers would give him the benefit of the doubt and put him into the highest category, while others would have preferred to watch him during a third term as Wales's captain and perhaps in New Zealand in 1977 before making up their minds. Certainly, however, there are few marks against him in the debit column. On the credit side, the first 'plus' is the fact that he took over a Welsh side that was rudderless and disorganised in early 1975 and led it straight to a European title, with only the one setback at Murrayfield. He also saved the selectors' blushes, for since the retirement from International rugby in 1971 of John Dawes the Big Five had revealed a strange unsureness of touch.

The appointment of caretaker captains – men like John Lloyd and Arthur Lewis, who were at the end of their careers – was followed by a year in which the command reverted to Gareth

Edwards, who had skippered his country in his rugby infancy and found the going hard. Gareth has his advocates, but it frequently seemed that he lacked the vital capacity to detach the mind from immediate problems and decide where his team's game needed tightening or where the opposition might next be probed. And this was understandable, since his position on the field was one where thinking-time is severely limited by constant and heavy pressure.

Some players, of course, did not want the responsibility of leadership. In 1972 the name of Barry John was being bandied about as a likely successor. But John has since admitted that he went to some lengths to avoid being invited to do the job. He feared that his own game might be inhibited as captain, and he maintains that he was not cut out for what he describes as 'the authority part' of being skipper — giving stern pep-talks to the boys.

One or two other men had strong claims backed up by a seniority calculated to gain respect. Gerald Davies, holder of twenty-nine caps by then and sometime captain of Cambridge University, was given the leadership of a Wales XV that played Tonga in the absence of the still-resting Lions who had been in South Africa during the summer of 1974. But he is essentially a quiet man, for whom communication with team-mates from an isolated post on the wing at Twickenham or Murrayfield might have provided considerable problems. Perhaps a similar argument weighed against John P. R. Williams at the time, and moreover, like Gareth Edwards, he had always apparently preferred to pour all his energy into his own game. Nor was there evidence that he had the will or the ability to direct others.

If we are talking about evidence, however, there was little to support Mervyn Davies as captain. As a teenager he once led a college XV and he had captained a Probables trial side in 1972 when Arthur Lewis was unfit: that was the sum total of his captaincy record. Nonetheless he was asked to lead the Reds in the trial of 4 January 1975, and a fortnight later given the reins for the roughest ride imaginable, before 50,000 screeching Frenchmen at Parc des Princes.

But John Dawes, the successor to Clive Rowlands as Wales team coach, had no doubt that this was the man Wales needed. Having been closely associated with Merv for six years he knew all about the iron will of the tall fellow with the mournful face and the black bandit moustache. He knew that he could lead by example. He knew that he had the authority which would both reassure the six new caps due to play in Paris and keep them on their toes. And he hoped that Merv had three or maybe four seasons at the top still in him, so that if he was a success Wales would profit from the continuity of leadership which she had recently lacked.

Other people had two main reservations. Mervyn Davies, they pointed out, was the team's primary ball-winner at the tail of the line-out, his full weight and strength were needed at scrums and mauls, and the attacks he initiated close to set-pieces yielded fast, clean second-phase possession. Was it fair to saddle him with the leadership also? The answer was given triumphantly in nine Internationals in which the Swansea man played some of the best rugby of his life.

The other question was simply about his personality. Could he dominate his XV and impose his will upon it? He appeared to lack the restless nervous energy and the gift of the gab possessed by predecessors like Rowlands and Dawes himself. Journalists knew that Mervyn was never one to thrust himself forward to the microphone or leap to answer Pressmen's questions. He often seemed withdrawn to the point of shyness, and if approached with a query might frown severely before delivering a brusque, no-nonsense comment. Other members of the Welsh side smiled readily and easily; the number 8 was serious of mien, and it often looked as if he was wearing the cares of the world upon his broad shoulders.

But there can be no doubt that the captaincy of his country encouraged a hitherto latent side of his personality to flower. During his two years as leader he slowly but surely became a man who talked fluently, if always thoughtfully, to those who asked his opinion. And it emerged that he did have opinions, strong uncompromising ones, about the rugby game and how it should be played, which he was anxious that people should understand properly. He gave clear, businesslike interviews to the media, which usually contained — to Pressmen's delight — eminently quotable sentiments and phrases. In short, the defence mechanisms he had devised to help him deal with fame and face the world were unlocked and the captain stood revealed as a man whose company and conversation were well worth having. Nobody was too surprised when BBC Wales signed him up after his retirement to assist in analysing the play at televised rugby matches.

And it goes without saying that his team, old hands and new caps, came to worship him long before his term as their leader drew sadly to its close. They at least have no reservations about 'Swerve's' claim to greatness.

MERVYN DAVIES

It was John Taylor who once said that if they ever made me captain of Wales he would have no hesitation in declaring himself unavailable for selection!

The remark was made years ago in a light-hearted conversation at Old Deer Park when a group of us were speculating about possible successors to John Dawes, who had just retired from the International scene. I prefer to think nowadays that John Taylor was pulling my leg, but at the time his threat struck home and confirmed the private belief I had at the age of twenty-four that I did not have it in me to lead a team.

For a start I did not consider my personality thrustful enough to inspire fifteen men to great heights and to crack the whip if they flagged. I felt that a captain should be a deep thinker on the game, the sort of bloke who could deliver an instant and articulate view on the state of play at the drop of a goal. I thought that he should be so smooth and charming that he would be super-popular among his team-mates. All characteristics that I didn't think I possessed – and that conviction stayed with me for several seasons. It was only when I sat back one summer and realised that I had collected nineteen caps that it occurred to me that if I stuck around for long enough my turn as skipper was almost bound to come!

And come it did, in January 1975. After Wales's poor showing in the unofficial Test against New Zealand the previous autumn, we sensed that the selectors were not too happy about entrusting the captaincy to Gareth Edwards in the forthcoming Home Championship. I suspect that Gareth would be the first to admit that as captain he did his own game less than justice. So much of the game depends on the expert functioning of an inside-half, and I think on reflection that it was asking too much of that outstanding player to hit top form in the cock-pit that is the base of the scrum, and to be sensitive to what was happening in other sectors of the field as well. Gareth was said to be disappointed at not continuing as captain, but I must add that under me he never spared himself in the service of the team. He turned in some wonderful games and scored tries when they were most needed.

But I had not been too surprised when in late November 1974 John Dawes, now our coach, sounded me out about the captaincy. Would I be prepared to lead the side? Did I think I could cope with the pressures?

Three years earlier I would not have been prepared for such questions, and my answers would have lacked credibility and conviction. By this time, however, as a seasoned International campaigner with twenty-nine caps and two Lions tours behind me I found that I had a philosophy of the game which enabled me to reply satisfactorily to John. I told him, simply and bluntly, that if I were the captain I would take Wales on to the pitch to win. Club games are for fun: at International level victory is the aim.

Nobody, I added, should expect to see Wales playing like performing seals under Mervyn Davies: if 50,000 people turned up to watch, that was their business. Once we had established a winning lead then they could hope for some exhibition stuff; but my first instructions to the backs would always be, 'We'll give you the ball — use it to get some points on the board.'

I also told John that I would expect my men to concentrate on cutting out errors from their game, but that if we were going to make mistakes in the nervous early stages of the play then I would try to make sure that they occurred well within our opponents' half, from which no damaging penalty points could be kicked. For his part, he reassured me that I commanded the respect of fellow Internationals; and that he was sure he and I could co-operate to the full as coach and skipper.

So, a few days after leading the Probables in the trial that followed, I was named as Wales's captain for our first game of the year, against France in Paris. Although I knew what was coming, it was still a startling and moving experience actually to read the word 'captain' after my name in the newspapers. Then, as if to dispel any idea that I might be dreaming, the congratulations and good wishes soon came pouring in, including a letter which I treasure from my own club, Swansea, who were doubly delighted, because in addition to Geoff Wheel and myself a third All White, Trevor Evans, would be playing against the French and gaining his first cap. My father was more phlegmatic about my promotion. 'About time, too,' he grunted.

This was the time when I realised that, though I had been holding it in check for years, my subconscious ambition had always been to captain my country. All rugby-playing Welshmen dream about it: first you aim for a cap, then to consolidate your place in the team, then perhaps for a Lions tour place. But the crowning glory must be to lead the men in red out to do battle for Cymru.

I gave thought, also, to my approach to the job. Captains seemed to me to fall into two categories: one could be like Dawes – a cold, calculating intellectual whose brain never ceased to work on the field. Not for Merv, I decided. My model would have to be McBride, a non-stop worker whose own play was a constant example to others. Furthermore, since everything a number 8 does is visible, the members of my team would be able to see that their captain was not shirking and would, hopefully, follow my lead. I decided, too, that like McBride I would cultivate a certain detachment and command-status to underwrite my authority.

However, I was also tormented by doubts, which lasted until the kick-off at Parc des Princes. I knew that as captain I should have to meet the Press and appear before the television cameras, but could I fence off the difficult questions and would my guarded comments satisfy the interrogators? Before too long I discovered that being interviewed was an art, which I doggedly set out to master. How would I fare, I also asked myself, when I had to deliver my after-dinner speech in Paris? Not being able to afford Muir and Norden as script-writers I employed the rival firm of Windsor and Wheel to prepare me a suitably eloquent address (they did!).

And of course I worried about the game itself, or more precisely the build-up to it. As captain of Wales I was allocated a hotel room to myself, but as I rested there on the eve of the match I wondered if I could get my players to take heed of what I would ask of them. John Dawes would be giving the important pep-talk the following morning, but I had responsibility for the final few words designed to motivate the Welsh XV minutes before we left the changing room.

So, carefully and laboriously, I wrote down on a sheet of paper every single thing I planned to say to my team, complete with underlinings and exclamation marks. It was, I thought, fairly powerful stuff! To my horror, when the moment came that I had to say my piece at Parc des Princes the next day I couldn't find my sheet of paper! I had to speak off the cuff, but thank goodness the words came somehow, and I got my message across. Never after that did I bother to commit pre-match thoughts to paper, preferring to speak as the mood took me and express my feelings spontaneously.

As some worries evaporated in the changing-room, so did others when we settled down to outplay the French. To say that the game was an easy one for me as skipper would be an understatement, but as we won by 25 points to 10 you can understand that I had few real problems. I must concede that the spadework these days is done by the coach, and a modern Welsh captain is his executive whose principal task is to see that the coach's directives are carried out during the play.

He may have to switch tactics occasionally, but if the preparation has been thorough and thoughtful the options are readily available. In that respect our generation is luckier than our predecessors, for I understand that success used to depend solely on the captain and what he could extract from his men on the day. I feel sorry for men who in the past had to lead out ill-prepared, ill-composed teams, and whose heads often rolled if they were unable to produce the desired result.

Never before or since, though, have I experienced the feeling of sheer elation that was mine as we left the Parc des Princes pitch (it was interrupted only when Geoff Wheel jerked my adhesive head-bandage off prematurely and very painfully in his attempt to give me a bear-hug of delight!). We had played splendid rugby, from the moment when Steve Fenwick, in his first International match, scored a try which gave us an early lead. This was exactly what I had asked for, since the French are always liable to become disjointed and depressed if you can put points quickly on the board against them.

Graham Price galloped three-quarters of the length of the field near the end for another first-appearance try, and in between Gerald Davies and Gareth Edwards contributed typical scores; but I recall with most pleasure the final pass I was able to give Terry Cobner, after we had swept the action away to the right for Gerald to step inside and link with his back row. It was great to have made people eat their words, including critics who had doubted whether we could hold our own, let alone win with one of the highest totals ever registered against France in Paris.

So I looked around the changing-room at fourteen weary but happy faces and said to myself, 'These are my boys – together we've done it!' I must confess, though, that I kept a little of my pleasure concealed, for I didn't want them to assume that they were world-beaters on the strength of one victory, however convincing. It was their job to win, so I contented myself with saying, 'Well done, we can enjoy ourselves tonight.' And we did just that!

Looking back I consider that the selectors are to be complimented on giving me a fine side to lead. True, it contained six new caps, but they were men of quality, whose tremendous enthusiasm and desire to win rubbed off on those of us who were more senior and less quick to get worked up. This was the first time, too, that Wales had gone in for 'unit' selection; that is, the whole of the Pontypool front row were chosen, along with their flanker Terry Cobner, while Wheel, Evans and myself were all Swansea forwards.

Sometimes I think it would have been great for the pack to contain a fourth All White to have strengthened team spirit and cohesion even further, but that is perhaps being unfair to that very accomplished lock from Aberavon, Alan Martin, the odd man out. In any case, our work as an eight left little to be desired, and I am sure that this was because club colleagues 'lifted' the morale of their team-mates and assisted them to play to their best form. If Bobby

Windsor is the hooker, Charlie Faulkner and Graham Price are going to make it that little bit more certain that no-one takes a strike from another 'Pooler player!

As captain I had to put one superstition behind me. Merv the Swerve had always taken the field last, and now I was having to go first. But when I led my side out at Cardiff in my second game as captain the last regrets about the change of routine were swept away by an avalanche of sound.

Fran Cotton took England out first to a roar that was almost terrifying. I didn't believe it could get any louder, but 50,000 Welshmen thought otherwise, and raised the volume by at least twenty per cent to greet us. It was a marvellously exciting few moments, and being at the front of it all, I liked to think, brought you a special cheer as captain of your country.

The crowd weren't quite so ecstatic at the end, for although we scored three tries and won by 20 points to 4 we allowed England to get up off the floor after the interval, when they trailed 16-0, and actually scored try for try with us in the second half. Certainly the English raised their game, and when Wheeler had to be replaced as hooker by the old warrior John Pullin it put fresh zip into their pack, but our supporters' instinct was right: we had lost a bit of control in the second forty minutes and allowed our opponents to pressurise us into errors on which they capitalised. We failed to rid ourselves of such mistakes in our next match at Murrayfield, where we went down to a defeat that I shall discuss in the next chapter – a reverse, however, that brought home to the newer members of the team that they were not invincible and that victories had to be worked for.

However, the Scots were the only side to beat us in a season which ended with victory in the match against Ireland and the 1975 championship title for my team. The amazing situation before that match was that Scotland could have won the title if they had won at Twickenham and we had lost. Ireland could have won it if they had beaten us and Scotland had lost. We would win it if we beat Ireland and Scotland failed to beat England. And, just to complicate matters, all three nations would have shared the title should we each draw! The stakes were high indeed, and certainly reflected in the tearaway Irish approach to the Cardiff match.

Rugby matches fall into three stages. There are the opening skirmishes, when each side sounds the other out; then comes the broad confrontation and the struggle to establish forward dominance; if a comfortable lead can be built up in that time, there may follow a third period when the ball can be run and the crowd pleased. Against Ireland in that 1975 game the 'confrontation' lasted a full hour, and it was not until then that we managed to break their stern challenge and play some colourful rugby. Gareth and Gerald continued their private try-scoring contest, John J. Williams and Bergiers scored once each and Charlie Faulkner smashed his way over for a first International touch-down. By then the Irish were resembling green-garbed rag dolls, but their resistance had only been sapped by sixty minutes of very hard labour indeed.

Since we would not be touring Japan until September, I was able to take a rare summer off in 1975. Some of it could be spent in mellow reflections upon a season in which we had taken a title twelve months before John Dawes's target date, March 1976. But it was also a relief to be able to devote time to family affairs. On 25 April, the second anniversary of Shirley's and my wedding, our son Christopher had arrived, and for once there was time to tackle just some of the problems involved in bringing up baby.

During my playing career Shirley had been a very understanding fiancée and wife. A Penygraig girl, I had known her at college, and our paths crossed again one day when I was in the Rhondda on business. During our ensuing courtship she wasn't a great fan of rugby and came to matches, she said, only because she liked looking at the boys' legs!

Later she became an ardent supporter of Welsh rugby at International level, though I don't believe the club scene has ever interested her quite as much. She has paid a price, however, for my involvement in the game. Sometimes she would suggest a visit to the cinema, only to find that training or a social engagement prevented our going together. There were male functions to which I simply couldn't take her, and even after mixed ones she occasionally admitted to having been bored at the non-stop rugby chatter. Again, the holiday that we snatched in Ibiza at the end of my convalescence in

1976 was practically the first we had taken since our marriage, for in previous years after returning from long tours I had not felt able to demand still more time off from my employers. All these things provoked occasional squabbles and friction between us, of the kind that I suppose most married couples have, but on the whole I must pay tribute to my wife's tolerance and patience during the high-pressure years.

I kept Shirley posted, as always, with news of Wales's Far Eastern Tour of 1975, from which we returned to begin an outstanding International campaign culminating in an Extra-Grand Slam. We began by disposing of Australia's challenge in a match that went completely according to plan.

After half an hour the important 'confrontation' period was over and we went on to demolish them. The kicking boots of Fenwick, Martin and Bevan were on 'beam-length', as Clive Rowlands would have put it, and Gareth got his inevitable score, but what pleased us most was John J. Williams's hat-trick of tries. The critics were saying that he had lost some of his shattering speed until he gave this crushing reply.

Although I have remarked that my term of captaincy contained few genuine worries, something that disturbed me deeply and unsettled the team as a whole as we prepared to meet England at Twickenham in January was the eruption of controversy surrounding Phil Bennett and the choice of the Welsh stand-off half. Around about the turn of the year Phil was bugged by a succession of small but painful injuries, and although he played one or two games for his club, Llanelli, he decided to withdraw from the WRU Trial, in which he had been chosen at stand-off for the Possibles.

It was after that that the Big Five dropped their bombshell. They omitted Phil not only from the Welsh XV but also from the thirty-one-strong squad, stating, 'Bevan will play against England and the replacement stand-off half will be David Richards of Swansea.' When pressed for reasons they added baldly, 'Richards is a better player than Bennett.' The whole of Wales, and especially the Stradey fraternity, could only shake its head in sheer disbelief. We at Swansea appreciated Richards's promise more than most, but to rate him in front of the recent British Lions stand-off half . . . !

It is possible that the selectors wished to discipline Phil for turning out for the Scarlets and dodging the trial. If so, why did they not do so privately, while covering themselves with a public statement that they were not satisfied with his general fitness for International rugby? Everyone knows how the situation was resolved by the subsequent injuries to John Bevan and Richards which led them to call on Phil after all for Twickenham, and he proved a big enough man to play a full part in the beating we gave England and keep his place for the rest of our triumphant season.

What about Llanelli's part in the affair? I will content myself by remarking that while selectors have the national interest at heart, clubs want their top men to appear as often as possible in the interests of winning rugby and attracting customers through the turnstiles. However, when International fixtures are in the offing, committees should give thought to players' feelings and allow them full recovery time from injuries, however slight.

You may be thinking that none of this was any of my business, and that it was a selectorial problem. I could not agree less. Since I had the greatest confidence in the abilities of both Phil Bennett and John Bevan, I would have welcomed the presence of either at standoff. But as captain what I did need to know well in advance, and with certainty, was which of them it was to be, for he would probably have to control tactics behind the scrum, call the moves for the backs and maybe function as vice-captain. So I was irritated by the selectors' lack of conviction, and also by Pressmen and members of the public wanting to know the truth or, worse still, belabour my ears with their version of it!

Months later it made me wryly amused to reflect that we had won a Grand Slam with the third-best man in Wales at standoff half!

Although Scotland scored first against us at Cardiff we soon got into our stride and beat them 28-6. So it was off to Dublin with a Triple Crown within our grasp. Before the trip I had a feeling that some team was going to suffer at our hands before long, and sadly for them it turned out to be the Irish.

Defeat was a bitter blow for them. Not only did we register a record victory of 34-9 for the fixture but we also caused a sickening setback to their build-up for a close-season tour of New Zealand (in the event they did not disgrace themselves out there, losing the Test by just 11-3). But they were gracious in their hour of misery, and it meant a lot to me when Mike Gibson commented afterwards that we were as good a side as the 1971 Lions.

Once again, mind you, the confrontation period was long and arduous, and at half-time when we led by only a point at 10-9 I had to give the boys a piece of my mind. They rewarded me with a purple patch midway through the second half when, in the space of five minutes, Phil Bennett, Gareth Edwards and Gerald Davies got tries to add to the one the last-named had scored early in the game, so that suddenly, with the help of some wonderful place-kicking by Phil, our lead had leaped to 25 points.

That day, too, I reached a personal milestone and overtook Denzil Williams's record as Wales's most capped forward. It was my thirty-seventh appearance for my country, but I still trailed behind Gareth Edwards, who equalled Ken Jones's overall total of forty-four caps in the same match.

I should like to deal here with a criticism that did the rounds at this time – that under me Wales were playing something called '35-yard rugby'. The implication was, I believe, that we were a safety-first XV, who declined to indulge in creative, imaginative rugby. I have admitted that I didn't approve of tossing the ball around until our lead became comfortable. But having said that, let me point out that we ran up no fewer than 102 points in the 1976 Home Championship campaign and scored 11 tries. You don't produce figures like that with safety-first rugby!

Perhaps the fans were complaining about a lack of excitement as our points totals soared into the twenties and thirties. That was not the fault of my team. The obvious needs underlining here – that excitement is at its peak when two teams are very evenly matched and nobody can predict who is going to win. Once the result becomes a foregone conclusion and it is clear that one team is going to emerge on top, then of course the excitement abates and spectators must settle for the exhibition-type rugby that the Welsh XV were able to play in the later stages of some of our games. The tension then vanishes and is replaced by spectacle, which I would claim we provided on more than one occasion. Ask the Irish.

Another carping criticism that we heard in 1975-6 was that although we were a good side, the standard of play elsewhere in Europe had declined, allowing us an easy ride to the top of the table. Why people should have said this sort of thing completely mystifies me, unless they wished to detract from the achievement of my team. If other teams were made to look poor when they played us, the critics ought to have asked themselves why. Did it never occur to them that fifteen Welshmen on top form had something to do with it? One day, I am sure, Wales will score the victory over New Zealand that has eluded us since 1953. Maybe on that occasion the cynics and moaners will shake their heads and declare, 'Ah, the All Blacks are not what they used to be.' Not Merv: I shall say, 'Who cares? We won!'

All in all, therefore, I was glad that our Grand Slam culminated with a victory over France for which we had to drive ourselves to the utmost and could show our true calibre. By late March we were a tired team, having had to gear ourselves up for one representative match after another since September. The French, in contrast, were going from strength to strength and were still very much in the title-hunt after wins against Scotland and Ireland. The match had been billed as one of the great games of the decade, and I am told that a television audience of about one hundred million saw it — no doubt ninety-nine million of them hoping to see this all-conquering Welsh XV humbled at last!

They had something to shout about soon after the kick-off when France scored off a handling error near our 10-metre line and Romeu kicked the goal. About the same time I suffered a painful haematoma or blood-bruise of the calf, and was sorely tempted to leave the field since I knew that it would get no better. But I did not want my side to be without their leader, and although the leg predictably got stiffer and stiffer I just managed to stay the course.

I was proud of the way the boys knuckled down to the job of eliminating our opponent's lead and remaining calm in the face of a furious offensive by the French which made the second half seem endless. They got a further touch down, which meant that for once we were out-scored on tries, but fine place-kicking by Bennett and

Fenwick, in addition to a good score by John J. Williams, pulled us through to a 19-13 win. For once, I feel sure, our fans were on the edges of their seats until the bitter end!

My memories of the afternoon include the ear-bursting roar that greeted Gareth Edwards as he led us on to the pitch to collect his record forty-fifth cap. Later there was the heroic tackling of John P. R. Williams which cut down Frenchman after Frenchman on the way to our try-line. John had scored the points which helped to win our opening game at Twickenham; in March he was a tower of strength at the other end of the field.

So I had achieved every International captain's aim and joined W. J. Trew, John Gwilliam and John Dawes as men who had led Wales to a one-hundred-per-cent successful season (and only Trew's record included a fifth victory like ours over a touring side). It's a great feeling, I fully admit, but at the same time I had excellent material to work with, and I take off my hat to the men under my command. Skill, strength, determination, guts, the capacity to keep cool under pressure — my team had all the virtues.

It is for others to judge my performance, but I should like to say two things about my contribution as captain. The first is almost gratuitous — but I think it is true that my height helped me to dominate situations and people when I needed to. At nearly six feet five inches, Wales's captain literally had to be looked up to! Second, I was in the best position to do the job: at number 8 you are closely involved in the forward struggle and yet sufficiently in touch with the halves to be able to influence back play.

As we came off the Arms Park after beating France, jostled and buffeted by our deliriously happy supporters, a reporter shot the question, 'What ambitions have you got left, Merv?' Off the top of my head I replied, 'To lead Wales to a hat-trick of Grand Slams.' And at that moment in time I had no doubt that it could be done.

Alas. Nobody knew it then, but for me it was the end of the trail.

5 Wales in Defeat

David Parry-Jones

For centuries Celts have been pushed around the place, first by Romans and later by Angles, Saxons, Jutes and Normans, all hell-bent on the acquisition of *Lebensraum.* Rather than risk confrontation with mightier forces, the Welsh would normally seek sanctuary in the high, inhospitable hills, sallying forth only occasionally to burn a castle or steal a few head of cattle. Such judicious bending in the wind has at least meant that Wales, unlike Scotland, has no history of immense numbers of her menfolk being butchered in bloody battles by the invader, and perhaps it is a strategy whose echoes can still be faintly heard in these more peaceable days: one day in 1972 after New Zealand had won a Test 19-15 at Cardiff, their captain Ian Kirkpatrick was moved to remark in the face of the home fans' rather reluctant willingness to face facts, 'You only score more points than Wales — you never beat them!'

It is certainly true that the modern Welshman has a built-in early-warning system of apprehensions and premonitions which used to be mirrored in the prelude to a rugby match in which his nation was engaged. He might have believed in his heart that his team contained heroes and demi-gods, but rather than admit subsequently that they also had feet of clay he invented a comprehensive defence mechanism of factors, some natural, some supernatural, which might in the event militate against a Welsh victory.

Notorious among them was the 'Twickenham bogy', who alone and unaided (you might think) by English players, allowed Wales to register only a solitary win at 'HQ' between 1910, when England first played her home games there, and 1950. He then clearly lost the magic touch and was pensioned off, only for his

Scottish cousin to take up residence in Edinburgh. The Murrayfield bogy took delight in casting spells over Welsh sides who were immeasurably superior on paper, like John Gwilliam's team of 1951 which plunged to defeat by 19 points to nil. There were, of course, malign gremlins at Lansdowne Road, and only our unfamiliarity with French mythology prevented belief in the existence of a hobgoblin who presided in the old days over Stade Colombes.

Other less arcane excuses framed to cover Welsh inadequacies included the wind whistling around the grandstands at Twickenham which was always liable to defeat the calculations of Welsh place-kickers (it being conveniently overlooked that English kickers did not often have the opportunity to perform at the ground either). The crowd at Murrayfield or Colombes would be radiating a special sort of hostility which would sap Wales's morale. A touring party possessed players whose ability really took them out of the human into the super-human category.

Such wild surmises allowed Welsh fans to accept defeat philosophically while holding on to the belief that their players were the greatest. And yet because there is usually plenty of natural talent on the conveyor belt here, this was a generalisation which down the years has had more than a grain of truth in it: witness the preponderance of Welshmen who have traditionally lent backbone to British Isles tour parties. But winning rugby is about far more than the mere presence of fifteen men on a field, and it was the lack of attention paid to basic organisation, selection and preparation which once formed a fertile seed-bed of failures by Wales in International matches which she ought to have won.

The wrong men were often picked, sometimes as a result of errors of judgment, sometimes because selectors were playing politics; they were chosen out of position or asked to play roles for which they were unsuited. New caps were flung into unfamiliar situations for which they and their team-mates were not prepared. A Newport wing can recall the occasion when he reported for his first International match, to find that the captain for the day knew neither his name nor his position.

Thus many decades of Welsh rugby history passed by in a relatively lackadaisical, disorganised manner. Sporadic victories were recorded over New Zealand, but every match against South Africa was lost. Only three times in the years between the wars did Wales take the championship title outright, and there was one stretch of forty years during which she failed to win a single Triple Crown or Grand Slam. Even in the immediate post-war years, when defeats were fewer, it is salutary to note that Cliff Morgan, for all his virtuosity, never played in a Triple Crown XV after 1952, when John Gwilliam was near the end of his reign as the Welsh captain.

Since the late 'sixties, however, the revolution of which Mervyn Davies was a part, with a team coach and squads, has meant the disappearance of uncertainty and slap-happiness from the Welsh approach. For a start the best available talent is now undoubtedly harnessed, and while you sometimes hear people saying that so-and-so ought to be in the squad it is rarely suggested that a player deserves to jump straight into the national XV from outside the squad altogether. The isolated errors made nowadays by selectors have less to do with choosing teams than with their own public relations (and on occasions perhaps they might display more readiness to explain themselves and their reasoning). There is a greater consensus in the rugby fraternity at large about who are the best players, and also more understanding about the aims and techniques of the Welsh side. Perhaps an intensifying of rugby coverage by the media in Wales can take some credit for the latter development. All this is good for the souls of Welshmen generally and the rugby scene in particular.

Its only drawback is that phen expectations are high, and belief in bogies and hobgoblins dispelled, defeat is a correspondingly bigger calamity and harder to swallow. A generation has grown up for whom Welsh victories are the norm, and the reaction of these young people, and the effect on the game at large in the Principality, are hard to predict should Wales regress into a lack-lustre or indifferent era.

For what has been the real reason for the scarcity of defeats suffered by Wales during Mervyn Davies's time? Some argue that it was his own outstanding ability as a player, allied to that of Edwards, John, Richards, Gerald Davies, Delme Thomas and J. P.

R. Williams; they expect that, with the retirement of the whole of this group of superstars, defeat is bound to become a more common occurrence. Mervyn himself prefers to think that the foundations of a proper approach to winning rugby have now been surely laid, and that defeats will still be rare events in future — provided that the lessons of occasional setbacks suffered by him and his contemporaries are understood and absorbed. That important reservation apart, I am inclined to agree with him.

MERVYN DAVIES

Fortunately in my time, because of good organisation and the outstanding talent we were able to call on, Wales lost very few games. There were two heavy defeats in New Zealand, about which I shall write later, but in Europe I was on the beaten side only six times for my country (seven if we count the unofficial Test against the All Blacks in 1974).

This was a relief in more ways than one, for my compatriots do not look kindly on teams that have gone down to defeat, and besides the endless inquests that take place in pubs and clubs, in the Press and on television, there is a lunatic fringe who invent an amazing range of excuses for their side's failure. They will announce that the referee was a crook or an idiot. They will allege that our players got drunk the night before the match, or that members of the team had a punch-up (yes!) in the dressing-room before the game. And they will puff their chests out and declare that, of course, had they been in the Big Five then such-and-such a player would never have got into the team at all.

And, don't forget, we Welsh players are very vulnerable to their verbal assaults. Our rugby community is so tight-knit and compact and intense that you cannot avoid being accosted — in pubs, in restaurants, walking along the street, even at the team hotel in the latter stages of a post-International evening when gate-crashers manage to penetrate the official gathering. Like most of my fellows I trained myself to be patient with bores, and I must admit that the Welsh XV devised a secret signal which indicated to alert teammates that an ear-bashing was in progress and rescue earnestly

1. *Making his mark for the first time: Mervyn Davies captains Swansea Training College in the 1967-8 season. Within twelve months he was to be capped for Wales*

2. *Protection for Gareth Edwards: 'I would select him ahead of Sid Going in an all-comers' XV.' Mike Roberts (left) watches, as does John Dawes from the midfield*

3. (above) *Wales, European champions of 1969, before departure for New Zealand. But they were no match for the All Blacks in the southern hemisphere. Soon Merv the Swerve (fourth from left in the back row) was to grow a moustache to give him a tougher image!*

4. (left) *Before a Test Match in New Zealand, 1971. The Lions pack prepares for the expected disruption from the All Blacks at the line-out*

5. (right) Mervyn leaves Heathrow Airport in 1971 en route for New Zealand as a British Lion. Cousins Joyce (left) and Margaret Drummond, BEA hostesses, escort him to the aircraft

6. (below) Domination of the tail of the line-out was a key factor in the 1971 Lions' winning strategy. Here Mervyn, supported by Dixon (left) and Taylor, frustrates New Zealand flanker Kirkpatrick

7. (left) *Pay attention, now! A PE lesson at Emanuel School*

8. (below) *Dai Morris (Neath), who played a record eighteen times with Mervyn Davies in the Wales back row, challenges Irvine of Scotland. 'Swerve' is at hand to cover a possible break*

9. 'The bravery needed to get in really low and avoid the flailing heels of the victim'— *Mervyn Davies about to take England's Ripley at Twickenham in 1974. Nos. 9 and 5 for Wales are Edwards and Robinson*

10. *After the final training session of the 1974 Lions before the first Test. Despite Ripley's challenge, Merv the Swerve has won the number 8 spot. Skipper Willie John McBride is fourth from left, standing: 'We'll take no prisoners,' his team were instructed by their coach Syd Millar*

11a, b, c, d. A try for the Barbarians v. New Zealand at Twickenham rewards tremendous support running by Mervyn. Gaining possession after a cross-kick he (a) beats Sid Going. Then (b) he shields the ball from Andy Leslie's grasp

before (c) driving strongly through the All Black's attempted smother tackle. Finally (d) he uses all his body weight to get to ground and claim the touch-down. Kent Lambert is too late with his support for Leslie

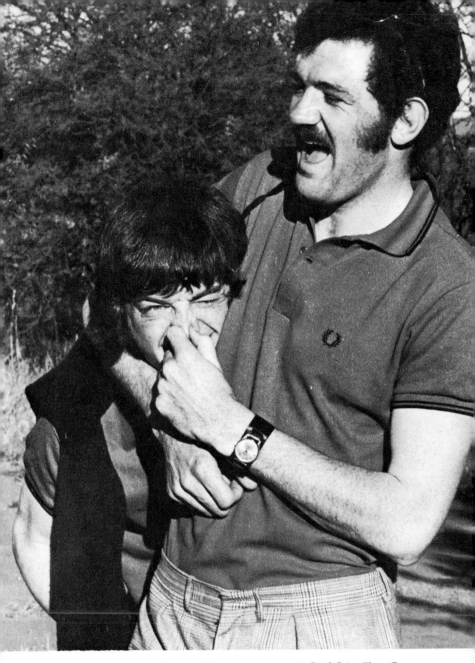

*12. Kruger Park 1974—Merv puts pressure on Irish Lion Tom Grace.
But soon the British Isles would be twisting the noses of the Springboks*

desired! Of course, too much enthusiasm is better than too little, so we all put up with it, but I have often envied Englishmen or Scots who can slink off into the comparative anonymity of London or Edinburgh after a beating to lick their wounds in peace.

For I must own up: defeat on the International field really hurt. Not that I lost any sleep over it, but perhaps I can explain my feeling by saying that my attitude to playing for Wales was that of a craftsman tackling a job of work, work that in my case was loved and gave great pleasure in being done well. So defeat simply meant that the job had not been completed satisfactorily.

There was a second sadness that I would experience: an awareness of having let Wales down. Although outwardly a cool customer I am, in fact, not ashamed to admit to quite a strong sense of patriotism. It has been with me for quite a long time, for even as a teenager I hated Wales to lose a game of rugby, or soccer or anything else for that matter. I expect that the feeling was imbued in me by my parents at first, but as I grew older I could recognise that their view of the Welsh scene was a true one: I came to like our people, their relaxed, agreeable approach to life, their friendliness, and their willingness to help in time of trouble, which was so vividly brought home to me during my time in hospital.

Wales's scenery, too, has a strong hold on me, particularly the beaches and mountains within reach of my native Swansea. I don't lose myself in the countryside to fish, as Gareth Edwards loves to do, but I share his view that the beauty of parts of our land can be important to a man's inner well-being.

It is true that I went off to London for a period. But I think I needed that experience to broaden my perception, and perhaps it helped to cement in me the conviction that Wales is one of the better places on this earth to live, especially compared to the great sprawling, noisy, crowded wen that is London. Anyway, I never had any intention of remaining in England and always wanted to come back to Wales, so that when in 1972 that great Swansea rugby family, the Blyths, offered me a position as a business representative back in my home city, I was both grateful and delighted. I felt that from a base in Wales I could make an even more effective contribution towards winning a place in the sun for

D

our small nation in the best way I knew – helping to achieve victory on the rugby field.

Hence for me personally, defeat for the men in red meant that Wales had somehow been short-changed by her chosen representatives. But having said that, let me add that I don't consider that I was a bad loser – on one condition: so long as it seemed we had gone down to a better side. And that, I ruefully reflected from time to time during my career, was not always the case.

Let us take some occasions when we lost, then, and try to analyse what went wrong. My first experience of defeat in Europe while wearing a red jersey was at Lansdowne Road in 1970. Our 14-0 beating was also the heaviest Wales suffered in the northern hemisphere in my time, and for only one other match was I in a Welsh side that failed to score. To say that it was a shock is an understatement, for were we not Triple Crown and title holders? Did we not possess some of the greatest players of their day? Had we not already disposed comfortably of England and Scotland? To the team and to the thousands of supporters who had crossed to Dublin, Ireland's win was a stunning, traumatic event.

Now playing against the Irish is never easy. Their fierce patriotism, combined with whatever is the Irish equivalent of *hwyl*, motivates the players – and allows their selectors to do extraordinary things such as restoring a veteran like Tony O'Reilly to the team at the advanced age of thirty-six. On that occasion Tony was to play against England at Twickenham, and at breakfast on the morning of the match he told his captain, Willie John McBride, of his fears that the fast young England wing opposed to him might be quick enough to run round him. Eying O'Reilly's waistline, which was advancing in girth like his years, McBride retorted, 'No chance. It would take too long!'

But seriously, Ireland's club rugby is far less intense and competitive than ours, so that their players remain fresher and are perhaps better equipped to pull something extra out for the big occasion. In my time their approach to a match has usually benefited from the intellect of Mike Gibson and the superb leadership of McBride. Yet their truly great players are few and far between, and on 14 March 1970 I am convinced that we fielded the better side.

But they whipped us. Why?

The excuses were legion. One of our players had thrown a punch at a team-mate in the changing-room and unsettled us: rubbish! The Irish had gone out to kill the rucks and deprive us of fast, useful loose ball: well, maybe. Some Welshmen had poor games? Thinking back I do recall that Barry and Gareth had off-days and that J. P. R. Williams made one costly error, but that does not excuse the rest of us. No side should ever depend on a couple of brilliant individuals to come good in a crisis and save their bacon.

No, our real enemy that day was complacency, which is fatal at all levels of the game and especially so in international rugby, whether it is Ireland who confront you or New Zealand or Japan. The Welsh side, at bottom, had the idea that having disposed of the English and Scots they would find Ireland a pushover and would not need to make a special effort.

How wrong can you be? That is why we could not put our game together. That is why we never touched top gear. That is why we allowed the Irish to make the most of the slender chances that came their way. And it all added up to a lesson I never forgot.

Something else I never forgot was the try scored against us by Ireland's number 8 that day, Ken Goodall. Everything seemed under control when Barry John chipped ahead within our opponents' half, and even when Goodall, covering behind his halves, caught the ball there appeared to be no cause for alarm. But the Irishman had spotted an empty area behind our fast-advancing three quarters, into which he swiftly delivered a deft kick ahead of his own. We still ought to have been ready for it – perhaps I should have been at hand myself – but to our dismay he streaked through our ranks, hacked the ball ahead and won a long race for the touchdown.

The points clinched the game for Ireland, and the try was as good an opportunist effort as I can remember being scored against Wales. Although it is always sad when rugby union loses a good man to the league game, I was not too upset about Goodall's move north later that year, for it removed a very strong rival for the number 8 spot on the 1971 Lions tour!

During my career the only European side to inflict two defeats on Wales was Scotland, who beat us at Murrayfield in 1973 and 1975. Although this also grieves me, since I invariably felt that we were a potentially better team than the Scots, I must say that Scottish sides are perhaps the most difficult of all to play open, running rugby against. The method they always adopted against us was a negative one consisting of pressurising us into mistakes, killing the rucks and mauls, and lying up as close as the laws allowed on our backs. Sometimes they even moved a flanker into midfield to assist their three quarters to defend, a job frequently undertaken by Nairn McEwan. On the other hand, who am I to criticise such tactics, since they manifestly brought the Scots the result they wanted more than once?

It was certainly the style which brought them the 1973 victory by 10-9, when they were also able to score two slick tries from within our 25. But I prefer to draw a moral from our experience in 1975. I know that injuries to Bevan and Fenwick disturbed our rhythm and that it was asking a lot of the replacements Bennett and Blyth (normally a full-back but perforce an emergency centre that day) to fit smoothly into a team which was being buffeted by opponents who had struck top form.

However, that is not my main grouse — it is the score-line which still saddens me whenever I look at it: Wales 10 points (one try, two penalties), Scotland 12 (one dropped goal, three penalties). In other words, Welsh errors cost us the game, for the great big boot of Douglas Morgan exacted long-range retribution for our offside and ruck offences. Since we have noted that one of the cardinal points of my rugby philosophy is, 'Don't make mistakes', you can understand that Merv had to hide a good deal of frustration and annoyance at the post-match dinner that night. Our errors also cost us more than a single match, since we won our three other fixtures that season and were soon robbed of a Grand Slam.

Mistakes, then, and complacency: to illustrate the third way in which you can go down to defeat while still considering yourselves the better side, I want to cite our beating at Twickenham by England in 1974. In my time England's record has puzzled everyone: in Europe they have been landed with the wooden spoon five times since 1969, and yet on tour they have scored victories over South Africa and New Zealand for which we Welsh would have given our eye-teeth!

This has led people to say, 'Ah, it's geography that defeats England — the sheer spread of her clubs militates against the achievement of cohesion and team-spirit. When her players really get together on tour she can still beat the world.' That sounds a fine argument until you remember that in New Zealand and South Africa the big rugby centres are far more distant from each other and those countries can still produce fine national sides.

I suspect England's administration may not be good enough, and likewise her organisation and approach to games. But I have no instant solution to offer. All I know is that in modern times, given present conditions, there is no reason why a Welsh XV should lose to England. Unless you come up against what we met in March 1974, indifferent refereeing.

John West, a relatively inexperienced Irishman, was in charge that day, and because he claimed to have been unsighted I am grudgingly prepared to forgive his refusal to award J. J. Williams a second-half touch-down that could have swung the game our way. People who had a better view, though, like Gerald Davies and those Englishmen closest to him, said that without doubt J. J. was first on to the ball.

Much more important in my view was his ignoring of the advantage law after Phil Bennett had pierced the England defence and a try looked certain. He recalled play to the ruck position, where he awarded Wales a penalty! Phil put the kick over, but it still meant that we had to be content with three points instead of a possible six to keep us in close contention. That was a bad decision. It was Clive Rowlands's last game as Wales's coach, and I cannot recall ever seeing a man quite so angry after a rugby match as he was when our boys trooped back into the changing-room.

Frankly, I am critical of refereeing generally at the present time. Many refs seem to me too long in the tooth, and out of touch with the spirit and the aims of the fast-changing modern game. Few of them are big enough to admit to mistakes after a match, and can always take refuge in a claim that they were unsighted at an important moment. I admit that refereeing is a difficult, thankless task, but I wish there were more men like Scotland's Norman Sanson, one individual whom I cannot fault. His virtues include a high degree of accuracy, the capacity to think like the players and understand what they are trying to do, and a readiness after a match to explain and defend any controversial decisions. I understand that he was a fine player in his youth, who had premature retirement forced upon him, but Scotland's loss has been refereeing's gain.

I am aware that the Frenchman Georges Domerq also has his admirers, but I believe that this is principally because he has controlled some spectacular games which pleased the crowds, like the Barbarians' defeat of New Zealand in 1973. So I don't rate M. Domerq much above average, nor do I consider French refereeing as a whole to be of a particularly high standard.

France, incidentally, scored just one win over us while I was playing in the Welsh side, but whenever we met them in the early days I had to acknowledge the problems they set us through sheer exuberance, with magnificent running and handling. In recent years, perhaps because of a desire to exert tactical control through the kicking of Romeu from stand-off-half, their style has become more predictable and easier to read. But I think that what French rugby needs above all is coolness and the ability to keep something in reserve for an emergency. Maybe they could have beaten us at Cardiff in 1976 had they possessed these qualities; instead, after being 6-0 down, we were the team who kept our heads and could pull out something extra when we had to.

I have suggested reasons why it is possible for a fine side to lose to opponents who were apparently less well equipped, but lest it be thought that Merv is peddling sour grapes let me admit that there have been times when I have felt sadly but realistically that Wales had been 'done' by a better team on the day. The two that stick in my memory (I might almost say in my gullet!) are our defeats by New Zealand in 1972 and by a New Zealand XV in 1974. Indeed, the only ambition which I never fulfilled in my career was to play in a Welsh side which beat the All Blacks.

There is no doubt that New Zealand are our arch-rivals, and have been since 1905 when Wales were the only XV to beat the First All Blacks. Equally, Wales are the country whom above all New

Zealand want to defeat, perhaps because at one time we held a 3-1 test match advantage over them which was not wiped out until 1969. So I can assure you that our preparations for the 1972 and 1974 meetings (even though no caps were awarded for the latter game) were the most demanding that I have ever taken part in outside a Lions tour. We may even have overdone it — I can understand the point of those critics who believe that on both occasions we were strung-up and hyper-tense when we finally took the field. Why else would a mature side like ours have conceded two elementary penalties in the first ten minutes against the '72 tourists? Karam's deadly boot put six points on the board, and from that point we were always attacking from behind. It is fatal to let New Zealanders get their noses in front, for they are natural winners and go from strength to strength.

I cannot say that All Blacks on tour are notable for socialising and small-talk, and they were not men with whom I held long conversations. For example, my great rival Ian Kirkpatrick (so big and powerful a flanker that the first time I set eyes on him I thought he was a lock!) is a quiet bloke, and in company we exchanged pleasantries rather than profound thoughts on the game. Perhaps his reserved nature is the reason why they took the captaincy away from him and gave it to Andy Leslie in 1974. Nonetheless, on both tours he was a dominant figure, a leader of attacks rather than the support player of earlier years. Incidentally we ought to have prevented his decisive try against us in 1974, just as we were suckers in 1972 not to have blocked Murdoch's touch-line thrust after Going's chip into the box which provided New Zealand's try that day.

'Kirkie' symbolised the whole character of the All Blacks' approach on tour, which confirmed the respect I have always had for them. They produced good, basic rugby with few frills, cut out mistakes, and played to their strength — a dominant pack. I must admit that their forwards held the whip-hand over ours in each of the matches I played against them for Wales. Perhaps one reason is that forward skills are hammered home to all New Zealand players from a young age. They could become flustered, mind you, and for the last twenty minutes of our Cardiff Arms Park tussle of 1972 they adopted illegal and obstructive tactics to prevent Wales hitting top gear and snatching victory. But it is to their credit that they held on.

Off the field the touring parties were held by some to be arrogant and even surly, and certainly back at the Angel Hotel after beating Wales they breathed an air of superiority as if they believed it their destiny to emerge victorious. However, perhaps some of that was only in the minds of the victims. When men are used to winning consistently, as Wales are too, they do make an effort to take victory calmly and undemonstratively. I prefer to see it this way: the All Blacks said to themselves, 'We came here to beat them. We beat them. What's all the fuss about?'

In any case, genuine rugby fraternity depends on mutual respect as well as on overt expressions of friendship. I do not remember ever exchanging more than a few words with the All Black hooker Tane Norton, yet, as I remarked earlier, it was he who took the trouble to correspond with me when I was in hospital in 1976.

So much, then, for occasional defeats. What about their aftermath? I must say that Welsh sides I figured in were pretty resilient and although we hated losing, it never played on our minds. As a sensible bunch of boys we used the hours after a game to ease any frustration and disappointment out of our system. Some players would do it immediately after their return to the changing-room, whose walls the intense young Llanelli centre Ray Gravell used to hammer with his fists. There was Charlie Faulkner, who came into the Welsh side late in his career and perhaps for that reason felt he had more to prove than the rest of us: in defeat he would slump on the bench and sadly but doggedly work out what had gone wrong, perhaps blaming himself because an opposing prop had given him some stick. It didn't happen often, but if it had then Charlie would own up. He is certainly one of rugby's honest characters.

From the changing-room we would struggle through the hordes of autograph hunters and make our way back to the team room at our hotel, where we had a tradition of spending a quiet half-hour or so reflecting informally on the game before the evening's entertainment and socialising began. Most of the players would have made time to pull on a dinner jacket before coming, though Derek Quinnell, the world's slowest changer, often arrived in casual get-up with hair still damp from the shower.

Only the serious beer drinkers risked being late, for this made people liable to swallow a pint of beer as a fine – usually committee men or selectors were the offenders! Then we spent the time paying restrained compliments to team-mates who had played outstanding games, or pulling the legs of those who had missed a tackle or dropped the ball. I remember toasting J. J. Williams for his hat-trick of tries against Australia, but the same bloke had to take some ribbing on an earlier occasion after he had dropped a scoring pass against England. We told him that his well-developed nose had obscured his view of the ball!

On reflection I believe that in victory or defeat such quiet gatherings were a valuable part of the fostering of team spirit for which we constantly aimed. They were always strictly private, and we had a reliable 'bouncer' on the door in that fiery member of the Big Five, Jack Young.

There would be the chance of a chat with the opposition at the post-match dinner, when I best enjoyed the company of other back-row forwards or half-backs with whom one could share one's thoughts on common aspects of the game. Roger Uttley, the Englishman with the well-lived-in face, was someone I liked sitting near, and there might be a referee or a Pressman with an interesting contribution to make. To hold conversations with visitors from France meant you had to draw on every last dimly remembered syllable of schoolboy French, though it was surprising how one's eloquence improved as the evening wore on!

Later on too, as proceedings became less and less formal, the boys would provide their own entertainment by performing their 'turns'. Early in my own career I was called upon for a solo, but since my singing voice is something like a foghorn it was agreed there and then that Merv the Swerve would always be excused in the future, so that I could sit back and appreciate a rendering of 'Galway Bay' by Willie John McBride or 'The big rock candy mountain' by John Taylor.

Derek Quinnell's standard offering was 'I did it my way', Arthur Lewis from Ebbw Vale liked singing rock-and-roll numbers remembered from his youth, while the big Neath forward Brian Thomas would boom out 'Trees'. Perhaps the most hilarious duet was Geoff Wheel, banjo, and Charlie Faulkner, vocals, with their version of 'There's a hole in my bucket' sung in drag — the crucial question was always whether Charlie could remember his lines. Gareth Edwards was our champion raconteur, who would illustrate some of his yarns with a deftly manipulated jock-strap!

Besides those who had taken part in the match, our replacement players often came into their own late in the evening. I suppose, for instance, that Mike Knill's hopes of becoming an International had receded a long way by the time he passed the age of thirty, yet in March 1976 he did dash on to the field for a first cap against France when Graham Price had to go off. Clive Shell once replaced Gareth Edwards under similar circumstances. These were men for whom the build-up to an International match was no less exacting than for the chosen fifteen players, yet usually they had to sit out the eighty minutes on the bench with no outlet for relieving the tension. So around midnight you might overhear someone like Roy Thomas of Llanelli, a replacement for Wales more than twenty times yet still uncapped as I write, suggesting *sotto voce* to Bobby Windsor, 'Surely you could get just a teeny-weeny little injury one of these days and let me on to the pitch!' 'Shunto' has been a great squad man for Wales in his time, and I always hoped he would get that elusive cap before finally calling it a day.

The drowning of sorrows, like celebrations, usually continued into the early hours and by the next morning, whether it was New Zealand or Scotland who had taken our scalps, the Welsh XV would have bounced back to something like normal spirits. After all, we told ourselves, in the long run rugby players are amateurs for whom the only price of defeat is a blow to the pride.

In our case, though, that did not mean any lessening of determination or dedication. My contemporaries in the Welsh team were thoughtful, intelligent men, willing and able to undertake self-criticism if necessary, and eager to co-operate with our coach to rectify any faults. So when we dispersed after a poor result from Wales's point of view we all knew that the next training session would find us totally committed to the idea that we were not going to have our colours lowered again.

Another thing we bore in mind was that if each International match is like a battle, the season as a whole is more akin to a campaign, in which you are out to finish above the other nations. A single setback doesn't mean that you have lost the war.

Once or twice during my International career Wales were obliged to share the championship title, including the unique tussle of 1973 when all five European countries finished with four points. But only in 1974, when Ireland were outright winners, did I play through a campaign in which Wales finished second to another nation. Only once, in other words, did we temporarily surrender that place in the sun.

6 New Zealand: The Darkest Hour and The Dawn

David Parry-Jones

Once upon a time, when the world was a smaller place, defeat was a bearable and forgettable experience for British rugby teams. Springboks and All Blacks might rampage through the land, scattering and squashing all opposition; but then they would retreat ten or fifteen thousand miles, leaving Wales, England and the rest to squabble over the spoils in a European fools' paradise. Sometimes a decade or more elapsed before the next wave of invaders arrived to teach a fresh generation of young Britons that they were no better than their predecessors. Pride, and wounds, had time to heal.

But the rugby era into which Mervyn Davies and his contemporaries found themselves launched was the jet age, in which Auckland lay but thirty-six hours' travel from Heathrow and the short tour was becoming a realistic proposition. Major overseas sides could arrive in Britain at the rate of two or three per decade to re-emphasise their superiority. British Isles parties went abroad twice as often as before — and returned just as inevitably with bleeding flesh and bedraggled Lions' manes.

Defeat, being more frequent, became less easy and more painful to live with. British rugby's shortcomings were more constantly exposed, and as the record of failure lengthened it became harder to hold the head high and pretend that the game in north-west Europe counted for anything at world level. The husky giants of the southern hemisphere would applaud the skill of English three-quarters or Welsh half-backs, before politely but pointedly referring their opponents to the score-line. World championships were exclusively fought for in series between New Zealand and South Africa.

During the first seven decades of the twentieth century it had proved particularly hard for the British Isles to do well in New Zealand. Dating from 13 August 1904, when the All Blacks won the single test of the series by 9-3, the Lions' record showed fifteen defeats, a couple of draws and one victory on each of the 1930 and 1959 tours. Sometimes the British sides complained that the host country's referees were harsh or even wilful; often the malign influence of goal-kicking was paramount, notably in 1959 when Don Clarke put over six penalties for New Zealand to pip the visitors, who had scored four tries, by 18 points to 17. But a quarter of a century later statistics never tell readers anything about such things or about glory in defeat — they simply show that, yet again, the British lost.

The last straw for the Lions came in 1966, when the touring party sent to New Zealand was undoubtedly brimful of talent. Its backs included Mike Gibson and the mercurial David Watkins, along with runners of the calibre of Bebb, McFadyean and Hinshelwood. Pask, McBride, Lamont and Telfer were members of a forward contingent who were confidently expected to achieve parity with their opponents. Alas! — the series result was a whitewash for what turned out to be the most dismal expedition ever to go down under. The story of the tour has been fully told elsewhere, and it seems clear that hard though the Lions tried on the field, organisation and preparation behind the scenes had simply not been good enough to cope with a major force in world rugby.

Perhaps the picture is slightly distorted by the fact that New Zealand was entering a period of exceptional attainment even by All Black standards. This was borne out during the 1967 tour of Britain by Lochore's party, who not only possessed the traditional strength at forward but also contained backs like Laidlaw and Kirton, who demanded that their country should play fifteen-man rugby, were capable of doing so, and were actively encouraged by their coach, Fred Allen. They won fourteen matches, including all the Tests, and drew a fifteenth. Their rugby was powerful and exceedingly good to watch.

The nucleus of that side was still available in 1969 when Wales, who that year had taken a Triple Crown and earned a draw in

Paris, went off on her first-ever solo tour of New Zealand. The odds were heavily stacked against the European champions for reasons that Mervyn Davies will make clear, but even the most sceptical of Welsh (or British) supporters could scarcely have foreseen that their heroes would return reeling from two successive batterings such as the men in red had rarely suffered since players wore knickerbockers and cloth caps.

That mauling was the factor which finally forced acceptance upon the British that, in spite of sporadic victories and isolated triumphs by individual combinations, their whole concept of rugby football, its aims and its execution, were in a different, inferior league from the game as it was played in the southern hemisphere. Ray Williams, as Wales's coaching organiser, was not in my recollection the first to articulate that idea; but he was the quickest to propose that there was no divinely ordained reason why we in these islands should forever lag behind.

New Zealand might have supermen who (so they told us) galloped up and down hillsides with sheep under their arms before tackling the less challenging problems posed by British visitors; but in the United Kingdom, reasoned Williams, there were keen, clever men who could become a match for their antipodean cousins, given the tutoring and the back-up. His enthusiasm caught on like wildfire — the patience and long-suffering of the Europeans had run out.

The Lions of 1971 were fortunate to come under the influence of two men who shared Ray Williams's vision and dearly wanted to give it reality. Their manager Douglas Smith was a solid, no-nonsense Scotsman whose cheery bonhomie disguised a ruthless determination to achieve the targets he set his side: two wins, a draw and one defeat — the All Blacks will never forget his near-astrological foresight! His assistant manager and coach was university lecturer Carwyn James, who had won a couple of caps for Wales at stand-off half, and was now coach to the Llanelli club. Of him it is sufficient to remark that he was but one of a legion of rugby men in Wales who had been outraged and appalled at what New Zealand had done to their country just two years before.

MERVYN DAVIES

Everybody knows those jokes about the 'good news' followed by the 'bad news'. As far as the year 1969 is concerned, for my career and for Welsh rugby, that formula sums it up perfectly. First, the good news: Merv wins his first cap and Wales go on to win a Triple Crown and become European champions. Next the bad news: on the New Zealand tour that summer we suffer two horrendous defeats, by 19-0 and 33-12. Suddenly and sadly, my friends, after a year like that, you grow up. You are no longer an innocent abroad.

We have much to discuss in this chapter, which is about plunging to the depths and rising to a great challenge. The wheel will turn full circle and there will be a happy ending. But since it is mainly about overseas events let me first say that in May 1969, at the age of twenty-two, Mervyn Davies was not the world's most travelled man. I had been to Germany on a school trip and there had been the quick flip across to Paris for the fourth game I played for Wales. That was the full extent of my foreign experience, and as for rugby tours – well, I had been with my college XV to Colwyn Bay, Bangor and Dolgellau, where the ale flowed sweetly and some matches were also played.

You can appreciate, therefore, that the prospect of going with the Welsh party on their summer tour of New Zealand seemed a marvellous one. I remember how fiercely we all played against France to try and ensure that our names would be in the tour list; we gained an honourable draw, and all fifteen players were invited to go down under, plus nine others. The full complement was: Brian Price (captain), Stuart Watkins, Alan Skirving, Keith Jarrett, Barry Llewelyn and Vic Perrins (a late replacement), all from Newport; Maurice Richards, Gerald Davies, Barry John and Gareth Edwards (Cardiff); Delme Thomas, Norman Gale and Phil Bennett (Llanelli); Brian Thomas and Dave Morris (Neath); Jeff Young and John Lloyd (Bridgend); Denzil Williams (Ebbw Vale); Dennis Hughes (Newbridge); Ray Hopkins (Maesteg); and four London Welshmen, John Dawes, J. P. R. Williams, John Taylor and myself.

To receive the invitation card was almost as exciting as winning a first cap. I remember calculating that as Wales were also due to play in Australia and Fiji I could hope eventually to have played against seven of the world's leading rugby nations within six months of my first International appearance. The sun was continuing to shine on my own career; and no clouds hung around the heads of the champions of Europe.

How did we view the New Zealanders? I cannot speak for the others, but as far as I was concerned the All Blacks were just another rugby outfit. I knew all about the rivalry with Wales extending back to 1905, but I was also aware that we had won three of the six tests hitherto played between the two nations, so there seemed no special reason for hang-ups or apprehensions. We were a good Welsh side, and maybe we could show the All Blacks (you have to be really on the inside of the rugby scene to qualify to call them simply 'the Blacks'!) a thing or two about open rugby. Some of the players senior to myself were more realistic about the likely calibre of the opposition, but I don't think a single one of us foresaw quite how hard we were destined to find it. In fact I remember some of us saying to each other, 'There are only two Tests — what a pity we are not going out for six weeks, when perhaps we could have fitted in a series of four.' Ignorance was indeed bliss!

Some tiny misgivings began at Heathrow when I climbed aboard the big jet that would wing us out to Auckland. I had to squeeze my six-and-a-half-foot frame into what felt like a three-foot gap, and was dismayed that this was to be my living-space for thirty-six hours. Big men like Ben Price and Brian Thomas experienced similar discomfiture and were grateful for the short break we got at Singapore.

So it was a group of bleary-eyed, dreadfully stiff young athletes who finally obeyed the air-hostess's command to fasten seat-belts and extinguish cigarettes for the descent to Auckland. I untangled my knees from around my neck and clambered wearily down the gangway, only to discover that our next two hours would be spent aboard a Fokker Friendship (a curious plane if ever there was one) that would fly us down to New Plymouth for our opening match against Taranaki.

We reached there at about four in the morning hoping fondly for a few hours' kip — when to our amazement we espied a throng of about two thousand frenzied New Zealanders who had got out of bed well before dawn and come flocking to the airport to welcome the Welsh, their country's arch-enemies of sixty-four years' standing. It seemed a pleasant gesture, and we expected that they would applaud us before allowing their visitors to slip away quietly for some rest. Not a bit of it! Swaying visibly from fatigue we were obliged to sing 'Sospan Fach' and the national anthem to them before we could board our bus and seek the sanctuary of our hotel.

New Plymouth was a bit like a cowboy town – a long street flanked by bars, hotels and shops – and I was not overwhelmed by its charm. Furthermore there was a sizable mountain frowning down on the place which, the locals told us, was covered by cloud except when the gods were angry. When we awoke and took a look around we observed that its peak was clearly to be seen – and sure enough within twenty-four hours I was in the middle of my first earthquake! The tremor made the windows rattle and shook our beds, further disturbing the sleep of Welshmen whose body clocks had already been sent wildly awry by a day and a half's flight across the world. Looking back I think that naked mountain peak was an omen for a tour that was ill-fated.

After a couple of light training sessions under our coach Clive Rowlands many of us were still in a daze when we took on Taranaki, just two days after our arrival. Ben Price and J. P. R. Williams scored tries, but I recall that we had to hold on to the ropes to get a 9-9 draw, and that the final twenty minutes were ab-solute purgatory. Before this I had been inclined to scoff at theories of 'jet-lag', but now I knew exactly what the experts were talking about. We must have been out on our feet – how else, I asked myself, could a mere New Zealand province hold the champions of the northern hemisphere to a draw? But if your legs feel like scrambled egg after an hour and you feel drained of energy, then you are brought up against reality and the need for total recovery-time after an inter-continental journey. Personally I felt some dis-illusionment – and more misgivings.

And then, a mere three days later, and still only five days after our arrival in New Zealand, we were facing the full fury of the All Blacks at Christchurch. Our hosts had been preparing for this day for months (if not decades!) and from the moment we hit the pitch we were up against opponents who were determined to rub our noses in the mud. I remember lining up for the anthems and noting with some concern that these men with ferns on their breast were the biggest that I had ever played against. An all-black strip, it is said, makes you look bigger to an opponent: these New Zealanders, men like Meads, Gray, Lochore and Kirkpatrick, really were bigger!

I have dwelt a little on the preamble to this Test match because I now share the view of critics who said that the fixture programme we undertook was suicidal. The flight out had been long and arduous, involving loss of sleep, and we did not get nearly enough time to acclimatise ourselves to the southern hemisphere. Perhaps we should have played the two Tests at the end of our visit; we could have gone to Australia and Fiji first, before tackling the demanding part of the tour in New Zealand. Either way, those who endorsed the schedule proposed by the All Blacks for Wales did not fully realise what they were letting the players in for. Next time our nation undertakes a short tour to New Zealand or South Africa I hope that these points will be borne in mind.

The result of the first Test was 19-0 to our opponents, who crossed for four tries, while we were lucky to get the 'nil'! I will take nothing away from them: observers say they were the best New Zealand side of all time, and who am I to disagree? They outplayed our forwards at line-out, scrummage, ruck and maul, all aspects of the play in which we truly believed we had improved no end. Our backs showed that they might have the beating of the All Black three-quarters, but were never able to prove the point on the meagre crumbs of possession we were able to offer them. So Lochore's side took us to the cleaners; it was men against boys.

However, while I am not making excuses for defeat, I will add that our first experience of Mr Pat Murphy's refereeing had not exactly endeared him to us. I considered that he awarded penalties against us for not releasing the ball after a tackle without giving us sufficient time to do so, so that Fergie McCormick was frequently able to gain huge chunks of territory for his side as well as put over a penalty.

The ironic thing was that Mr Murphy need not have set out to teach us a lesson. The rake-rucking by the All Black pack soon taught us not to lie around after going to ground with the ball. I was once rucked ball and all, to emerge on the New Zealand side of the loose scrummage under the frowning gaze of Sid Going. All in all not a pleasant thing to suffer!

One down, one to go. There followed demanding provincial engagements against Otago and Wellington, which we won well. Against the latter side we showed our teeth in a brawl which erupted five minutes before the end of proper time, causing the referee to blow prematurely for the end of the game to save the Wellington forwards from a real going-over. After the drubbing we had received from our hosts' national XV these were genuinely encouraging victories, and although I cannot say that we oozed with confidence we felt prepared to give the All Blacks a run for their money in the second encounter.

June 14, 1969 – complete disillusionment: Wales 12 points, New Zealand 33. Although Maurice Richards scored what was handsomely acknowledged to be the cleverest try seen in the country for many a long year and Keith Jarrett's kicking was closer to its normal quality, down we went again. Our pride was broken, our self-esteem shattered. Only one other Welsh XV had conceded more points since the dawn of the century. We felt inadequate, we felt sick, we were glad it was all over.

The main executioner that day was our opponents' full back, McCormick, who scored a record 24 points with the boot. I salute Fergie's accuracy; but when in his recent biography he cites Pat Murphy as the best referee he ever played under I am lost for words.

Let me quote two examples to indicate my own rating of Mr Murphy. First, after one of McCormick's successful place-kicks this amazingly patriotic official leaped high in the air with delight as he blew his whistle!

Second, I was penalised by him under these circumstances: Barry John found touch ahead of the forwards, and as the Welsh pack moved up to the line-out Malcolm Dick flipped a quick throw-in to Brian Lochore, whom I put down very hard. Mr Murphy blew for offside against me! In retrospect such naivety in a referee would be funny, except that at the time it was nothing short of tragic. In 1976 I read how the All Blacks had bleated about the alleged short-comings of South African referees, and I smiled to myself. This was how we felt in 1969. I hope that neutral referees will soon become the rule in the southern hemisphere as they are in Europe.

Stories, I know, came back to Wales about our party's failure to knuckle down to the business of winning the Tests, and people said we had not tried hard enough. I shall be blunt. The younger members of the team, John P. R. Williams, Phil Bennett, Barry Llewelyn and others had a good tour and came back with reputations enhanced. I also felt an honest contentment that I had given of my best, and if I suffered delayed shock for some months after our return home, then it should be remembered that in 1969 I was a mere rugby stripling, who had never before experienced anything like the sheer physical commitment of an All Black pack in full cry. That acid critic Terry McLean referred to me as 'the lean bean', but was good enough to add that I had done well.

What must be said is that we younger tourists felt rather non-plussed when, after the first Test, some of our older players appeared to throw in the towel and settle for an easy ride through the final three tour matches in New Zealand. It seemed as if they had decided that, as they were nearing the end of their playing careers, there was little to be gained from going flat out and taking a battering during the remaining fortnight. That was their business; but it is not an attitude that would nowadays be tolerated from anyone presuming to wear the three feathers of Wales.

In some ways, then, I prefer to forget the playing side of my first visit to New Zealand. I shall always remember the All Blacks' hospitality, though. All of us were treated like princes, and nothing was too much trouble for our hosts. Their favourite guest was, we thought, Ivor Jones, who made the trip as President of the Welsh Rugby Union. He had been a member of the 1930 British Lions down under, and everywhere he travelled in 1969 there seemed to be representatives of the older generation falling over themselves to remind him what a great player he had been, and how he had once run 40 yards to send in a team-mate for a quite magnificent try. In this and other ways it was brought home to us that although rugby is almost a religion in Wales, the New Zealanders are if anything more fervent and devout than ourselves. And in 1969 they got their human sacrifice – the Welsh touring side!

It was a relief to move on to Australia, where I felt sad to see how rugby union is a poor cousin to league and Australian Rules football. Furthermore the Wallabies were not as strong on the field as they had been when defeating Wales at Cardiff in 1966, so that although the Sydney Oval pitch was a quagmire on the day of the Test we pulled through by 19-16 and felt that our reputation had been restored just a little. The Aussies could have tied the game, though: when Arthur McGill crossed for a try Maurice Richards gave referee Ferguson a bit of 'lip', and had the ball been lighter, Arthur might well have punished us with the subsequent penalty from half way.

The visit to Australia was memorable for one other incident from the Welsh point of view. Gerald Davies, already at that time a brilliant centre but rather slight, had been neutralised as an attacking force in New Zealand by big centres running at him with the ball and seeking to take him out of the action with heavy tackles. For the Sydney match we switched him to a wing, from which he duly scored the first of his incredible sequence of tries for Wales and the Lions. That was a clever bit of creative thinking by our coach, Clive Rowlands.

We rounded off our trip with a few days in Fiji, where 24,000 people turned out to see us defeat their team by 31-11. This was the sole representative match for which I took the field as a lock, with Dennis Hughes at number 8 – I prevailed upon him to swap places at half-time! Wales were very sharp that day, particularly our centre Keith Jarrett – and maybe the frogs which had invaded our training area the previous day had a lot to do with our nimbleness. There must have been literally thousands of them, hopping and croaking their way between the touch-lines, and I have seldom seen Keith go to such lengths to side-step his way through any defence!

The Welsh XV met royalty in Fiji in the shape of King Ratu. The height of the palace's esteem for us was demonstrated by the presentation to our manager Handel Rogers of a Whale's Tooth, such as only Queen Elizabeth II had received before. Mind you, we put ourselves out to visit the King; he lives on an island, to which we were being rowed in a dug-out canoe when the heavens opened and our craft nearly sank with the volume of rain-water. As it was we got soaked to the skin, but the change of clothes with which we were provided included skirts instead of trousers. I suppose that I looked comical enough, but the fancy-dress prize was undoubtedly shared between John Lloyd and Ben Price, whose calves looked anything but shapely and glamorous between their borrowed lower garments and their rather rumpled socks. An obligatory swig of kava juice, the ceremonial drink which Fijians brew from grass roots, made people feel worse rather than better!

We struck up some good friendships with the Fijian players, some of whom we were to greet subsequently when they toured Wales. The boys decided that Ilaitia Tuisese and I were actually long-lost twins — his height and frame are uncannily like my own, though he has by far the better sun-tan!

Our expedition, then, ended on a happy note. Nothing could dispel the fact that the pride of Wales had been rudely punctured down under — but at least we now understood the true strength of the enemy. The New Zealanders had shown us what we had to beat, the standard we had to reach by 1971, when many of our party hoped for an invitation to join the British Isles tour. We realised how limited were our forward skills compared with theirs, and particularly it came home to us how merciless was their exploitation of second-phase possession.

For my younger readers I must pause to explain that it is not so hard to plan a defence against attacks from set-pieces like scrums and line-outs; once, however, the opposing forwards have gone stampeding into your midfield, taking out two, three or more key defenders, then you are far less capable of dealing with the next wave of attacks. You have tacklers lying on the ground, out of the game temporarily.

In addition to the second-phase lesson, I personally acknowledged how rapid had been the New Zealanders' arrival on the loose ball, when they were always fractionally ahead of us in the battle for possession. Also, although I had no pretensions to place-kicking myself, I realised how vital it was for a team to field a man who could be guaranteed to put over a high proportion of penalties and conversions in a Test match; Keith Jarrett of whom so much had been expected, contributed but six goal points in the Tests.

In the two intervening years before the Lions tour I reflected often upon these lessons. At first I was always pessimistic, but then tiny grains of optimism began to take root, since it was obvious that other Welshman who had shared my ordeal at the hands of Lochore and co. had done their bit of thinking as well and decided what had to happen to our rugby if we were to do well in 1971.

As a result, I have no doubt, Wales enjoyed two very successful years, culminating in the Grand Slam clinched in Paris – and that was just before John Dawes, the captain, myself and eleven team-mates were called to Eastbourne for a week's preparation before leaving to represent the British Isles in New Zealand. A second confrontation with the 'Blacks' was in the offing!

The routine side of preparing for a Lions' tour is rather tedious. For a start there is public relations, which at Eastbourne involved our signing some four thousand autograph sheets. Signatures got less and less decipherable, and the names of Mickey Mouse and Desperate Dan often cropped up in the later stages of a long session.

We also had to meet the tailor, and although everyone had sent measurements in advance it was amazing how many big bony wrists or spindly ankles protruded from sleeves and trouser legs as lanky blokes like Gordon Brown, Delme Thomas, Mike Roberts or Merv the Swerve had a first fitting for their tour apparel. We each got two blazers, the 'number one' in black with a small badge and the 'number two' in dark blue with a bigger badge for dinners and formal occasions. My generation stands on its dignity far less than its predecessors and is not so keen on club ties, badges and blazers (there are seventeen of the latter in my wardrobe, though I wear one only rarely). However, for a tour party, I think it pays to dress neatly and uniformly, and our spruce appearance must have contributed to the fantastic team spirit we were to achieve.

The sports goods manufacturers were on hand, pressing us to sample their products, and most of us took advantage of their presence to accept and break in new pairs of boots. As a man who regularly went through three pairs of size elevens per season I was one of the particularly grateful recipients.

We trained at an Eastbourne school pitch which was rock-hard, and I feel sure that most of us held back a little lest a broken ankle or wrist sustained in training should rob us of the trip of a lifetime. That is one reason why I felt that if Lions tourists are to have a week of preparation and special training then it ought to take place once the destination has been reached. With fears of being left behind dispelled, the coach is bound to get a better response to his demands. Kitting-out can always be fitted in somewhere along the line. We lost our first game in 1971 against Queensland because of the old enemy, jet-lag, which we could have conquered in Brisbane instead of hanging around in Britain. So it pleased me that by 1974 the Tours Committee had seen the wisdom of sending the Lions out to South Africa for a full week before the first fixture.

However, Eastbourne 1971 was not without its advantages. We certainly broke the ice and got to know each other well. The Welsh contingent quickly learned to appreciate the dry humour of Scots like Ian McLauchlan and Gordon Brown. There was the canny know-how of the Irish, even though McBride and Lynch often disguised theirs behind a haze of pipe-smoke that followed them as far as the touch-line! Englishmen like John Spencer and David Duckham came out of their shells, while I trust that the other nationalities realised how the Welsh, albeit intense and serious about their rugby, could laugh and joke and mess around like the rest of them. As senior International players we had known each other as opponents for three or four seasons; now we were learning to become compatriots for a few months, sinking our respective national prides into a British consensus of loyalty.

The build-up of confidence, so vital among men who had felt the lash of New Zealand power in recent years, was intensified by outsiders who sought to help forge us into a united party and motivate us. From the Welsh Rugby Union, Ray Williams came to tell us of his recent coaching trip in the All Black strongholds, and promised us that there were chinks in our opponents' armour which our coach would help us to exploit. His was an inspiring address, and the sole

occasion that I can remember when Carwyn James was actually up-
staged for an hour or two.

Carwyn himself was little known to me, for although he had won
himself a high reputation in the homeland as a thinker on rugby my
own first-class experience in Britain had been gained in London. So
I viewed this coach of ours with almost as much reserve as some of
the Irishmen and Scots, who wondered what manner of man would
be ordering them around for the next fourteen weeks. We knew that
Carwyn had master-minded a West Wales XV that had given the
Sixth All Blacks a good game, and that he now coached the Llanelli
club — but before that it seemed that his main experience had been
with the First XV of Llandovery College, a public school in the
Welsh hills! He was the possessor of two Welsh caps; but Wales
had not asked him to coach their national XV. Was he any good?
Or was he in the long line of ineffectual, bumbling pukka sahibs of
British rugby?

It was at Eastbourne that it dawned on all of us, at roughly the
same time I should think, that Carwyn was not only a brilliant
analytical thinker and tactician, but also a superb listener only too
ready to capitalise upon the knowledge and ideas of others. His
own understanding of the rugby game was already encyclopaedic,
but we soon noticed how during training periods he invited contributions from specialists like McBride and McLoughlin, revealing
an astonishing capacity for selecting what he thought was useful
from the comments of his players and injecting it back into collective team performance.

He would devolve responsibility for some ploys to Willie John,
or John Taylor, or John Dawes, or myself, analyse whether they
were potentially productive, and précis their essence for the benefit
of the team at large. And after training, clutching a gin and tonic
and puffing his fiftieth cigarette of the day, he would still be ready
to hear ideas, absorb them, and discuss how they might further our
mission — to beat New Zealand.

I do not suggest that all his virtues became immediately apparent
at Eastbourne, but we sensed them and began to realise that we
were in capable hands. It was the same with the admirable Dr
Douglas Smith, an unknown quantity to most of us, even his fellow

Scots. He had toured New Zealand as a Lion in 1950; but would he prove too abrasive and aggressive, we wondered uneasily, to be a good tour manager? A caustic Scottish sense of humour, laced with short, sharp Anglo-Saxon words of advice, had a few of us blinking with disbelief at first.

But in that first week Doug founded the reputation he was to enjoy by the end of the tour – as a great players' manager. He took the pressure off John Dawes and Carwyn by dealing courteously and firmly with the British Press, and spoke crisply and with authority in public. In training we found that he would always lend a hand (a dreaded punishment for a lazy Lion was to carry the manager's 14 stone the length of the pitch). As the matches came along we found that he could set the seal on Carwyn's basic motivation of our chosen XV with a final few fiery words calculated to impel us on to the field determined to smash everything in sight. Yes, at Eastbourne Doug gave notice that he would be a refreshing character to have around.

All in all, a good week's preparation, probably better than anything that had ever gone before. As I squeezed my large frame into one of those excruciatingly small airliner seats at Heathrow, I remember thinking that perhaps after all we had a party that could lay the giants low. Even though we lost that pipe-opener in Queensland and had difficulty in defeating a New South Wales XV 14-12, I still felt that the All Blacks would have to look to their laurels to hold the fifth British Lions.

Time goes by and the dusk of history is already settling around the great campaign of 1971. So I think it is worth cataloguing the membership of the party which left Britain that summer managed by Dr Douglas Smith, coached by Carwyn James and skippered by John Dawes.

It included six Englishmen: Bob Hiller, Dave Duckham, John Spencer, Chris Wardlow, John Pullin and Peter Dixon; half a dozen Irishmen – Mike Gibson, Ray McLoughlin, Sean Lynch, Willie John McBride, Mick Hipwell and Fergus Slattery. There were six Scots: Alastair Biggar, Sandy Carmichael, Ian McLauchlan, Frank Laidlaw, Chris Rea and Gordon Brown. The other twelve of us were Welsh: J. P. R. Williams, Gerald Davies, John Bevan, Arthur Lewis, Barry John, Gareth Edwards, Raymond 'Chico' Hopkins, Delme Thomas, Mike Roberts, John Taylor, Derek Quinnell and myself. 'Stack' Stevens joined us as a replacement for Sandy Carmichael half-way through the tour, and Geoff Evans came too, bringing the final London Welsh contingent up to seven. Very gratifying for the folk at Old Deer Park!

In spite of the hiccoughs in Australia, by the time we arrived in New Zealand, to a reception from a thousand enthusiastic Aucklanders, we had been welded into a potentially most formidable unit. I cannot put my finger on one particular reason, but I realised that a combination of circumstances seemed to have given us an aura of confidence that even our hosts were quick to recognise. The Eastbourne foregathering, the assuredness of our management, the belief generated in our own capability — these were factors which helped us to think from the start in terms of winning. That, as you now know, was the kind of outlook which suited me down to the ground.

Another factor behind this mental attitude was the presence of men who had lost too often and too heavily against New Zealand. Like all the other Welshmen I hungered to avenge our humiliation of 1969, while Irishmen like Willie John and Mike Gibson spoke so sourly of the taste of defeat that we almost wanted victory for their sakes alone. We were, indeed, a body of men bent on vengeance.

I seriously doubt whether British players had ever previously gone abroad with such single-mindedness. But it should not be overlooked that evolution within the game itself had also moved the odds in our favour. The Australian 'dispensation' rule had been adopted, making it harder for half-backs to kick for touch at will in front of their forwards, and encouraging the running game and counter-attack.

These were already broad British ideals, but ones that had been embraced particularly fondly at the London Welsh club by John Dawes, ironically because of the relative weakness of our pack: at Old Deer Park the backs, rather than waste any possession, however indifferent, would move the ball from positions that other clubs considered suicidal, such as our own in-goal area. It was frequently profitable, as Carwyn James was coincidentally proving at Llanelli. So it became the Lions' basic approach to the tour, one on which captain and coach were straightaway in total agreement.

While, therefore, important reassessments and rethinking about the game were taking place in the home countries, what had happened to New Zealand rugby in the two years since the Welsh visit? The blunt answer is, nothing.

The All Blacks, I have emphasised, were and still are the ultimate exponents of second and third phase attack. The loose ball was the all-important commodity: as long as it could be won at rucks and mauls, then New Zealand half-backs could always clear their lines or, better still, send in back-row forwards or midfield players for tries from short and medium range. Here was a rugby machine which had worked for decades, defying the successive challenges of British and other invaders. Why meddle with it? It would work again.

This blindness to change elsewhere was not confined to the All Blacks' rugby hierarchy and their coach Ivan Vodanovich. In our early days down under, as we moved from reception to banquet to party (we suspected that a fifth column was plotting to undermine our fitness, so lavish was the wining and dining!) it further became clear that the New Zealand public was no more than politely sceptical about our chances. 'We're sure you'll put on a brave show and entertain us very well,' they told us. 'But you'll be no more than gallant losers at the end of the day.' What they did not appreciate was that rugby in the British Isles had suddenly become an attacking game, and that the last thought in our minds was that we had come as chopping-blocks for All Black packs. We were in their country to win matches.

It is not my intention to chart the tour fixture by fixture, but the victories we chalked up in our first five games are worthy of note because of the super-charging effect they had upon our already buoyant spirits. Thames Valley Counties, Wanganui King Country (where I got the first of my five tour tries), Waikato and the Maoris were all sunk without trace, and this stage of our visit culminated in a superb 47-9 victory over Wellington in which we crossed the line nine times. Of course I did not see anything of the Wellington XV subsequently, but it is said that overnight they switched to a 'Lions' style of rugby and finished their season as holders of the coveted Ranfurlie Shield.

Dominant personalities in our team were emerging by now, and although Barry John and John Bevan were stealing the headlines with their scoring feats, behind the scenes two players were exerting enormous influence. One was, of course, John Dawes, who besides continuing to be the cool, unflappable captain I knew well at Old Deer Park, was busy showing New Zealand his superb all-round skills in the centre.

Before the tour the (English?) Press had been suggesting that he would find it hard to win a Test place against the challenge of Spencer, Rea and Gibson assuming that Barry John became the first-choice stand-off half. I even had small doubts myself, but they soon evaporated as 'Sid' began to turn in performances that were a model of consistency. As a post-match speaker he was often a soothing influence after the provocative stuff Doug Smith would let fly.

Another whose outstanding contribution we acknowledged was Ray McLoughlin. What an organised, methodical bloke he turned out to be. Besides pulling his weight as a superb front-row technician he sought to bring direction to our pack by insisting that the backs relay their next ploy to the 'donkeys' so that we could support them to the full.

Thus code-words like 'post' (the ball to be kicked directly up-field) and 'kox' (the ball to be kicked into the 'box') were relayed at set-pieces from Barry John via Gareth Edwards and myself to the men at the front. Sometimes it must have sounded like the calling of witnesses at a court of law! But this was the way Ray introduced a spot of discipline if he thought Carwyn had us on too loose a rein.

A splendid tour companion, Ray had to have everything worked out. Even in that game beloved of rugby men, liar dice, at which he was cunningly expert, he never gambled. 'It's the odds ye need to know,' he would assure us — and ninety per cent of the time he was dead right! He will also be remembered by chefs and waitresses the length of New Zealand for his craving after tins of fruit salad, which he would down at a gulp whenever he felt peckish.

Ray was, of course, one of the casualties of Canterbury, the most notorious event in stage two of our tour leading up to the first Test. The Lions won a game which, since I sat it out in the stand, I have no hesitation in ranking as the most vicious and ugly I have ever seen. And because I know that our boys did not take the field that day bent on thuggery and mayhem, I place the blame fairly and squarely on the Canterbury players. Kicking, trampling, punching – they pulled out all the unpleasant tricks which distinguish the unacceptable face of rugby football, and it was a supreme test of character for my fellow tourists.

McLoughlin broke a thumb retaliating for a blow he was struck at the end of a line-out, while Sandy Carmichael incurred a multiple fracture of the cheek-bone. Both men had to pull out of the tour; the same fate befell Mick Hipwell, while the walking wounded at the final whistle were John Dawes, Mike Gibson and Gareth Edwards. John Pullin, our hooker, was also stretched out at one point by a savage upper-cut.

The opposition full-back that day, Fergie McCormick, has written that the Lions did not emerge from the game smelling of roses. I agree that British rugby players are not angels, and I myself have been none too fussy over the years about methods used to subdue the opposition, but I draw the line at Canterbury's approach. That evening was the first post-match occasion when our boys declined to mix easily and amicably with the opposition. We preferred the company of those Pressmen who were openly advocating that Canterbury should be omitted from future tour schedules.

However, I must say one thing more about the Canterbury experience: outside the Tests it may have been the biggest single event which cost New Zealand the rubber. The Lions' resolve to beat their opponents, even without two men who had been earmarked as likely Test props, was immeasurably stiffened at Christchurch.

We now knew the full extent to which All Blacks might go on the rugby field to ensure themselves the victory: very well, we would match it, if necessary. 'Get your retaliation in first' was the provocative slogan that emerged from our camp, but Canterbury can take the credit for demonstrating to us that every man jack had to look after number one. It did not help New Zealand's cause when one of their officials promised us a massacre akin to Passchendaele in the first Test the following week-end. He may or may not have been knowledgeable enough to know what he was really saying, yet these were words which could not help but raise our head of steam even higher.

Mind you, we had ways of softening up the opposition too, less brutal and crude than Canterbury's, but far more subtle. Something that troubled the All Blacks throughout the Test series was Doug Smith's allusion to the 'weak link' in their line-up. This was a veiled hint which drove New Zealand's Press and their supporters frantic in efforts to discover what he was driving at. I cannot reveal the secret, for the manager told none of us either! Even Carwyn James has since admitted that Doug kept him in the dark about it. So I conclude that it was simply a shrewd bit of psychological warfare.

For three weeks before the first Test I had suffered from what the doctors said was a 'groin strain', which deprived me of match practice. Although I had kept up my training I wondered whether the selectors would risk picking me at number 8 when they named their XV for Dunedin, a week in advance of the game. It was one of the highest compliments I have ever been paid to find that I was included in the team, even though it was agreed that I should still have to miss the Tuesday game against Marlborough-Nelson Bay. The other candidate for the position was Peter Dixon, and although some eyebrows were raised when he was chosen as a flanker I consider my selection was right. Let me explain why.

For Wales in 1969 I had a fair bit of success in neutralising a tactic that was immensely important to New Zealand, the securing of possession at the end of the line-out followed by a ferocious peel into midfield to commit the opposing defence. My height and relative lightness (I was still under 15 stones) made it possible for me to get really airborne; and again in 1971 I knew that I would possess this advantage over the probable All Black back-row men Kirkpatrick, Wyllie and Sutherland who were neither as tall nor as agile as I. It lay within my power, therefore, to deprive our opponents' attackers of part of their basic diet.

Carwyn James completely shared my view that this was vital to the Lions' strategy, so the ability to dominate the tail of the line-out was something I was trying to perfect when my illness brought a temporary interruption. However, when the chips were down I had the height, the weight and the experience, and on the day I was a good risk. Peter Dixon, incidentally, fitted splendidly into his allotted back-row role.

We trained with added zeal and purpose during the week preceding the Test, and one of the pleasant features of it all was the whole-hearted co-operation given to the chosen XV by the shadow men. The reserve forwards played in practice as we believed the All Blacks would, in order that our pack could perfect counter-ploys, particularly to the disruption we anticipated at the line-out. Chico Hopkins became Sid Going for a few days, at the end of which even he was moaning about the merciless way in which John Taylor, Dixon and I hammered him into the ground when he broke close to the scrum! He finished up black and blue – but chirpy as ever.

They say that ten thousand spectators were locked out at Dunedin on the day when, for only the third time in history, the British Isles won a Test match on New Zealand soil and, like their predecessors in Ivor Jones's year, went one up in the series. Forty-eight thousand people, though, did see McLauchlan score a try and Barry John kick two penalties, to which the All Blacks could reply only with a McCormick penalty goal. Those, however, are just the statistics. What the score-line does not reveal is that for Merv the Swerve and probably fourteen other Lions this was the hardest, most demanding game of a lifetime.

Let me admit frankly that we spent much of it with our backs to the wall. Some of New Zealand's giants of recent years like Tremain, Gray and my number 8 rival, Brian Lochore, had retired. But their successors on 26 June 1971 were cast in true All Black mould, and just as furiously did they hurl themselves in dark, rolling waves at our try-line. But somehow, for eighty long minutes, the thin red barrier held. Somehow? It was sheer bravery and guts that pulled us through, for in most aspects of the play we were well-nigh annihilated. But the word had gone round: 'They shall not pass.' So, time and time again, big men like Sutherland, Meads or Muller would thunder their way towards the target, only to be stopped in their tracks by superb tackling. John P. R. Williams stood out, but nobody dodged his duty and even Barry John never shrank from pitting his eleven stones against the bulk of forwards almost twice his weight. Chico Hopkins, too, who came on to the field when Gareth Edwards's hamstring muscle became too painful for him to continue, also covered himself in glory.

Although I found the savagery of the New Zealand assault awesome, I must say that in one way it was my kind of game. One good tackle gives me more pleasure than ten tries, so I reckon I enjoyed myself to the extent of a thousand tries at Dunedin! Always on hand were Dixon and Taylor, and never has a defensive trio in which I played got through quite so much hard work.

People say that the Lions abandoned their free-running approach that day and took refuge in ten-man rugby. That may be true: but we simply had to. Our possession ratio was, I suspect, the lowest of the series, and most of the time Barry and Gareth were having to use the ball to kick us out of trouble. Before the Test we had demonstrated one rugby virtue which we possessed — the capacity to attack, attack and attack once more. Now, under enormous pressure, we had shown that we could also defend, defend and defend again.

New Zealand's captain Colin Meads was quick to call at our changing-room afterwards to congratulate us on our win, but deep inside he must have been baffled beyond measure at his team's inability to capitalise on their superiority around the field and score more points than the Lions. One obvious reason was the way Barry John's accurate tactical kicking had made McCormick look a monkey all afternoon, unsettling him so much that his place-kicking was below par and he missed chances which could have tied the scores. But if Colin had taken the trouble to ask the delighted Doug Smith or Carwyn James or John Dawes, they could have told him the real difference between the sides: the will to win of the 1971 British Lions.

We had taken everything New Zealand could throw at us and emerged with heads held high. However, although in my opinion

E

we played better rugby in the second Test at Christchurch, where we got more of the ball and Gerald Davies scored two tries, we lost by 22-12. At the time, as tourists, we were going through a slight trough and were not at all keyed up. So when Ian Kirkpatrick pounded away for a 60-yard try that ranks as one of the best I have ever seen, and when our opponents were awarded a penalty try for a tackle by Gerald on Bryan Williams that was adjudged premature, most of the stuffing was knocked out of us and we never really got back into contention.

The penalty try, incidentally, was the ruling of John Pring, who refereed all four Test matches and was considered by the Lions to be the best available official in New Zealand. He was not perfect, and some of his decisions puzzled our boys, but having been scathing about Pat Murphy I must place it on record that we found Mr Pring absolutely fair and impartial.

Clearly, with nine hard fixtures remaining, which included two Tests that would decide the nicely poised rubber, we now needed breathing-space in which to rethink, to rebuild our resolve, and to rediscover that will to win. The opportunity came immediately after the second Test, when we spent a leisurely week relaxing at the holiday resort of Queenstown in agreeable scenic surroundings. The place was almost deserted except for thirty-odd young Lions determined to enjoy themselves even in the middle of New Zealand's winter. For a few days we could put aside a life-style that involved eating, sleeping and living rugby football, and indulge a few simpler tastes common to ordinary tourists.

So we polished up our choral renderings, and made sure that we integrated newcomers 'Stack' Stevens and Geoff Evans into all social activities. And although we are remembered as a reasonably well-behaved party, we took the chance at Queenstown to let our hair down, make a bit of noise and sink a few quarts of ale. Pranksters came to the fore, notably Arthur Lewis. On one occasion he, Derek Quinnell and myself were ascending to a mountain-top hotel on board a chair-lift car shaped like a large half egg-shell. Near the top 'Asia' pulled a lever, whereupon a wide panel, used to let rain-water out, opened up beneath Derek and myself, who looked down aghast at the tops of pine trees many feet below. Arthur, who may have been after a place in the Test back row, fell around with laughter, but we two were not amused.

Another development that took place within the party at this time was the realisation that, in contrast to the early days when our management had gone to great lengths to emphasise our basic unity, we now comprised a Test or 'Saturday' XV and a 'Wednesday' side, our supporting cast. However, this in no way affected team-spirit; rather, it led to some humorous and healthy rivalry. For instance, Bob Hiller, rechristened 'Boss' as a result of his inspiring leadership of the Wednesday team, ruled that socially, at least, his men were far superior to the Test players, and to join our team-mates at certain exclusive functions we lesser mortals had to produce a printed invitation card. 'Boss' also conferred honorary membership of the Harlequins RFC upon Chico Hopkins, who accepted humbly and said he didn't believe this could have happen-ed to many folk from Maesteg.

Bob Hiller (and to be serious for a moment, don't forget that this splendid tourist notched 102 points in his eleven appearances) was but one of a crop of players who sprouted nick-names: Gordon Brown became 'Broon of Troon' (his home town); John Taylor was 'Bas', short for Basil Brush, the television fox-puppet, a rather obscure joke about the length of his hair; Sidney John Dawes, of course, had long since become 'Sid' to all and sundry, to distinguish him from others by the name of John in the rugby game; while I answered to 'Swerve'. It rhymes, naturally, with my abbreviated Christian name, but it actually derives from an answer I once gave to a journalist's silly question: 'How do you beat a man?' 'Well, I sort of swerve around him,' I replied lamely — and it stuck!

We really appreciated that Queenstown week, for although sub-sequently in South Africa I was to discover that there are a few easy games, this was not true in New Zealand. But despite the fact that Doug and Carwyn wisely let us relax for a day or two, they were soon demanding fresh commitment and dedication and reminding us of our basic mission, to defeat New Zealand.

After a quartet of victories in provincial games we went into the third Test at hurricane force, and within twenty minutes had built up an unbeatable lead which turned into a win that meant we could not lose the rubber. Barry John dropped a goal, Gareth Edwards fed Gerald Davies in for a try on the corner flag, and finally the two halves combined beautifully for Barry to score at the posts. The 'King' slotted two conversions, and although Mains got a try for the All Blacks, the final score was 13-3 in our favour.

The critics said that after that dynamic first quarter of the match, we had sat on our lead and permitted New Zealand to get back into the game. But that 13-3 scoreline is proof that we had done just enough early on, for the play levelled off as our opponents recovered from the shock treatment they had received. Not for the first time I felt satisfaction at having denied the All Blacks possession at the end of the line-out; moreover, this was a fine vantage point to sniff their forwards' unease, discomfiture and finally panic as time ran on without their being able to cut back our lead substantially – and then ran out.

Brian Lochore returned that day to partner Colin Meads at lock when Peter Whiting was declared unfit. But he just did not offer at all, and I considered that his country had done a grave disservice to this once-great player when they pressed him to emerge from semi-retirement to face the Lions.

More provincial victories followed, including an 11-5 win over the Going family concern, North Auckland (for whose team three Goings appeared), in which we were often hard-pressed to hold on. But by this time there was only a week of the tour left, and I am sure you can appreciate that it was hard to keep our minds entirely clear of the re-unions that soon awaited us with families and loved ones. Early on, our manager had forecast two wins, a defeat and a draw in the Tests for his men, so perhaps in the fourth Test we settled for that 14-14 score line to prove Doug's psychic powers!

Nostalgia had perhaps ousted the will to win as our primary emotion, and in the last week on New Zealand soil we could often be heard singing our rendering of 'Gee but I wanna go home', harmonised to the tune of 'Sloop John B'. Nonetheless, we found the courage to recover from an 8-0 Test deficit at one stage, and Peter Dixon's try, J. P. R.'s dropped goal and the two penalties and conversion by 'King' John earned us a share of the spoils – and a history-making series victory!

It was a wonderful feeling and we celebrated hard, but my goodness, it had been tough going. Never over a period of fourteen weeks have I had to put up with such severe and sustained mental and physical discomfort. On my arrival back at Heathrow my parents and other members of the welcoming party remarked on how pale and drawn I appeared. But it didn't matter: to have been part of the greatest British rugby combination of all time was more than compensation. As the first Lions to win in New Zealand, we knew that we were guaranteed a sort of immortality!

Earlier in this book I have written of the All Blacks in victory, with that air of total superiority which they wear as of right and not immodestly. In defeat, on their own soil, many of them were completely shattered. A few New Zealanders were, perhaps, relieved that the long record of success against visiting British sides had been smashed, with a corresponding release of tension. Most, however, did not know what had hit them and were uncertain how to face such a strange experience. Sid Going, a surly little man at the best of times, was among the sourest in defeat.

I should except Colin Meads from this criticism. New Zealand's captain gave full praise to the British Isles and although defeat in front of the home crowds must have hurt (as it did me in Wales), 'Pine Tree' pulled out the right phrases and voiced correct sentiments as he paid tribute to our achievements. On the very last evening in New Zealand I remember seeing him sitting with Chico Hopkins on his knee, the pair of them fooling around like a ventriloquist and his dummy! Not much is wrong with our game of rugby when that sort of companionship can manifest itself at the end of a hard-fought campaign.

My trip, the second one down under, had indeed proved the tour of a lifetime, with the added satisfaction of having scaled a rugby Everest. In my opinion the feat had always been within Britain's grasp, but in the past the preparation and the mood of our players had been all wrong. You have to believe in yourselves before you can overcome the enemy on his own ground. Carwyn James had coached his side into breaking a credibility barrier.

Sadly the Lions split up at Heathrow and again became

Welshmen, Englishmen, Irishmen and Scots. Soon, we knew, we should once more be spitting hostility at each other as our separate nations battled again for European supremacy. But the memories lingered on, both in the numerous receptions and reunions we all attended, and later when my trunkful of souvenirs and tour mementoes, sent from New Zealand by ship, caught up with me. Maori craft-ware and trinkets bought the length and breadth of North and South Islands with carefully stretched pocket money reminded me of wonderful days spent in Tauranga, Gisborne, Blenheim, Invercargill and the other great centres of All Black rugby football.

Yet already it was all in the past. The Lions could not consider themselves on top of the world until they had beaten off the other great southern hemisphere challenge that 1974 would bring.

Could we prove ourselves the tops again, this time in South Africa?

7 *Hunting the Springbok*

David Parry-Jones

Cardiff, December 1960: a bleak winter Sunday, with Cathedral Road and parts of Sophia Gardens swirling darkly under overflow water from the River Taff after rain which had bucketed down incessantly for the previous twenty-four hours. The rugby pitch over at Cardiff Arms Park, never quick to drain in the best of circumstances, lay flooded to a depth of 9 inches.

And yet a day earlier, in soaking swamp-like conditions which could hardly have been more different from the dry, bouncy grounds of Transvaal and Natal the Fifth Springboks had powered their way to a 3-0 win over a Welsh XV which ought to have been far, far more at home in such Atlantic coast weather. South Africa, playing with the storm in the first half, led by only a penalty at the interval; but the narrow lead had just sufficed at the end of a second forty minutes during the whole of which they clamped the home pack in a bear-like embrace beneath the North Stand. The Welsh forwards were denied the possession which might for a few vital moments have offered their potentially superior back division a chance to penetrate the midfield and get a touch-down or two.

In its own unspectacular way it was a virtuoso performance, exactly right on the day, serving to confirm the view held by a post-war generation in Wales that whatever problems New Zealand might set, South Africa was really Top Nation at rugby football. Nine years before, Basil Kenyon's side had come to the principality with magnificent players like Muller, Koch, van Wyk and Brewis and defeated a Welsh XV which, at that time dominant in Europe, had registered a Grand Slam in 1950 and was to repeat the feat in 1952. Their manager Frank Mellish admitted that the 6-3 victory owed something to luck — likewise the 11-9 defeat of a Cardiff team which was then basking in a golden era — but many who saw his team still find it difficult to conceive of a better balanced, more effective touring party. When the first post-war New Zealanders lost to Cardiff and Wales two years later the verdict was simply confirmed: good as New Zealand might be, South Africa was the country which set standards the others had to reach.

The validity of this estimate, incidentally, is borne out by the results of matches played between those two nations right up to their series of 1976. That was a campaign which brought the All Blacks only a single victory to add to the twelve previous ones over their green-jerseyed rivals. South Africa's three successes advanced her total to nineteen. Looking nearer home, although Wales had scored three victories out of nine full Tests against New Zealand, she had lost six out of six encounters with the Springboks until 1970 when a late try snatched a draw at Cardiff, again in conditions which were more suitable for reptiles than young athletes.

Inexorably, then, over nearly three-quarters of a century, South Africa had built up a position of pre-eminence in the rugby world; the chance of a tilt at her representatives was a prospect to be savoured by any who wished to test themselves against the very best opposition the game could offer.

Meanwhile, however, the policies of successive governments in the union were causing her increasing unpopularity and isolation from the rest of the world. The venom of Britain's anti-apartheid demonstrators manifested itself constantly during the Springbok tour of 1970, when nails and broken glass were sprinkled on rugby pitches and the players' hotels menaced by bomb threats. Not only were the demonstrators opposed to the presence of a South African party in the home countries; they also considered that by playing against the tourists, British players were somehow 'giving comfort' to the South African régime, or were even helping in a malign way to do down the Union's black population.

For its part the rugby fraternity was unimpressed by the frenzy of groups of agitators, seeking to influence and manipulate its freedom to indulge in social and sporting intercourse with whatsoever folk it chose. Indeed, there was vigorous reaction, and demonstrators squealed with dismay as they were forcefully and sometimes painfully removed from pitches which they sought to invade. On the other hand, it is only fair to add, not much ice was cut by the idealistic clap-trap mouthed by right wing defenders of sporting contact with the Springboks, who talked of 'bridge-building' and the desirability of impressing upon young South Africans the impeccable political morality of the United Kingdom.

It is a fact of life that most rugby people are apolitical where the 'game' is concerned. Those with a liking for dialectic told the demonstrators, 'as long as we trade with South Africans, why may we not play against them? Go and protest to the government.' But to the majority the link between sport and politics, as defined by intellectuals, meant little. All players are viewed simply as human beings, more or less expert in a specific field of endeavour. For better or worse no attempt is made to judge the ethics of the administration under which they live. Hence South African rugby players tend to be seen in the same light as East German swimmers, for instance, Russian athletes and gymnasts, or Spanish footballers.

And the aim is a simple sporting one: to challenge and if possible defeat them. That is what governed the British players' wish to compete against the Springboks in 1970 and subsequently the resolve of the Lions to undertake the tour of 1974, whatever political forces might seek to dissuade them. And the desire of Mervyn Davies and the rest was heightened by awareness of the statistics cited above: the British might beat their chests and boasts of the James–Dawes achievement in New Zealand until they were blue in the face, but only victory in Cape Town, Johannesburg, Durban and so on could round off their claim to be world champions. It was the natural wish of the sportsman, in other words, to beat all comers.

So although the government frowned and announced that the British Isles side could expect no invitations to embassy parties while in South Africa, the 1974 tour went ahead. And perhaps, after it was over, more people than cared to admit it were glad that rugby men had beaten hell out of the exponents of apartheid rather than taken cover behind political slogans to suspend fixtures. Minister of Sport Denis Howell was not at Heathrow to wave

them goodbye; but he was there when they came back with the
spoils of victory.

MERVYN DAVIES

During my early rugby career, Press notices had been perfectly fair
to me, though I sometimes wryly reflected that they had not touched the level of eulogy accorded to my more glamorous contemporaries like Barry John and Gareth Edwards. Forwards, it seemed,
were still rated as a mere service industry. But I discovered in 1973
and 1974 that this could cut two ways. That was the period when I
consider that I played my most indifferent rugby, by the high standards I set myself – yet I was never carved up or pilloried by rugby
writers. I conclude that their powers of observation are not always
what they are cracked up to be, and that they didn't really notice!

I myself, though, was uneasily aware that I no longer looked
forward to International football with the same keenness and
appetite. On the field my commitment was less than total, and
probably the application that went into my play was slightly
diminished. The reason was connected, I supposed, with the score of
appearances I had by now made for my country and a feeling I had
in my bones that Merve the Swerve was unlikely to be dropped.
There seemed few genuine challengers around for my position as the
best number 8 forward in Wales, and I had no real doubt that I
would be selected for the British Isles side bound for South Africa.

Thus I was resting on my laurels and badly in need of some fresh
motivation and stimulus. In this chapter I shall explain how it took
an Englishman to spur Mervyn Davies back to his very best form,
and to enable me to participate in yet another epoch-making rugby
tour de force.

The Lions' party did, as I anticipated, include my name, but a
number of men who had been key players on the New Zealand visit
of 1971 would be missing. 'King' Barry John had retired; Hiller,
Dawes, John Bevan, Delme Thomas, McLoughlin and Geoff
Evans of London Welsh were no longer in contention for various
reasons; while Gerald Davies, Dave Duckham and, initially at least,
Mike Gibson had declared themselves unavailable. However, my
experiences three years earlier suggested there was every reason to

suppose the selectors would have assembled the best possible side, and I looked with satisfaction at the thirty-strong list.

In addition to myself it included eight Welshmen: J. P. R. Williams, John J. Williams, Clive Rees, Roy Bergiers, Phil Bennett, Gareth Edwards, Tom David and Bobby Windsor. Scotland supplied Andy Irvine, Billy Steele, Ian McGeechan, Gordon Brown, Sandy Carmichael and 'Mighty Mouse' McLauchlan. From England there were Geoff Evans (of Coventry), Alan Old, Andy Ripley, Tony Neary, Chris Ralston, Roger Uttley, Mike Burton and Fran Cotton, while from Ireland came Tom Grace, Dick Milliken, John Moloney, Stuart McKinney, Fergus Slattery, Ken Kennedy and the captain, Willie John McBride.

As Ireland were the current European champions and Willie John was their skipper, his appointment to lead the Lions seemed logical and perfectly acceptable. The big lock had been twice previously to South Africa, in 1962 and 1968, so his experience would be invaluable. Personally I rated him as a hard-working, honest craftsman of a forward, whose views on the way the game should be played coincided with my own, and I had no doubt about being able to give him the hundred-per-cent loyalty he would demand. For one thing, I could listen to his Irish brogue all day long!

It also seemed sensible that, just as the James–Dawes Welsh axis had worked so well in 1971, we were now to have an Irish partnership guiding our fortunes on the field, for our coach was to be Syd Millar, McBride's old Ballymena club-mate. Alun Thomas, from my own home town of Swansea, who would manage the party, was a third man who already had experience of South Africa, having been there with the 1955 Lions and again with Wales as an official on the 1963 visit.

Compared with our week at Eastbourne in 1971, we spent but thirty-six hours assembling in London – at a venue so secret that I cannot remember its name! The official reason for this brief pre-tour preparation was the desirability of reaching our destination as rapidly as possible in order to acclimatise ourselves to playing at altitudes where there was less oxygen in the air. I approved of this after the traumas of 1969 and 1971, so could not complain about the short period of time allocated to kitting us out with tour uniforms. The only real casualty was Roger Uttley, whose blazer and flannels fitted only where they touched, and who was told by his fellow Englishmen that he resembled the comedian Norman Wisdom!

However, our anxiety to shun the limelight derived from political pressure that had been brought to bear on us, both collectively and as individuals, to decline the tour invitation and thus make a gesture of protest against the South African government's apartheid policy.

Like a number of other players I had received letters from political agitators and religious leaders suggesting that I should withdraw. The letters went into the bin, for I must declare that politics interest me little beyond their effect on the price of cigarettes and beer. Don't get me wrong: I realised that apartheid was controversial, and that my old London Welsh team-mate John Taylor felt so strongly about it that he had refused to play against the 1970 Springboks. But I differ from him in my view that sport and politics do not mix. I had always been prepared to play against anyone who promised to provide good opposition and a hard game of rugby, no matter what creed they held or what colour was their skin. Furthermore, although our government might attempt to persuade us not to tour, in the end they could not forbid free men the right to choose those against whom they wished to play.

Finally, I felt that the tour would give me a chance to see apartheid for myself. You do not, of course, have to see a shark savage someone to know that it is a mighty dangerous creature; but broadly speaking, I think first-hand experience always makes for better understanding than hearsay.

In truth, although there was concern that demonstrators might molest us if it were known where we were foregathering in London (though only one or two of them came to jeer us on our way at Heathrow), I had other things on my mind, in particular my potential status within the party. The other number 8 chosen by the Lions was a tall, spare character from Rosslyn Park called Andy Ripley. He held sixteen caps, was as tall and heavy as I, and undeniably faster, and had scored a neat try under the noses of our back row for England against Wales that January. He had followed this up with good performances against Scotland and France.

The Press had even been hinting that on the hard, fast grounds in

South Africa he might be better suited to the Test back row than myself. At that pre-departure reception Carwyn James told me, 'Merv, you'll have your work cut out to keep that fellow out of the reckoning.' Carwyn was undoubtedly seeking to put me on my mettle, but at the time I failed to spot any twinkle in his eye, and viewed Andy with growing concern. Did this chap present a serious threat to my Lions Test career? It was a new feeling to have a rival in the camp.

Not long after we flew into Jan Smuts Airport to an ultra-enthusiastic reception (for South Africans had feared that the tour would in the end be cancelled), the vital need for a full acclimatisation period was brought dramatically and painfully home to me.

Although I am not the world's most energetic chap, I trotted out willingly enough for our first training session at Potchefstroom in Western Transvaal. It lay about 5000 feet above sea level, over three times as high as Ebbw Vale, which was probably the loftiest town in which I had previously played rugby. Our practice ground included two rugby pitches, around which Syd Millar asked us to jog in order to warm up. No trouble at all.

It was as we began the more strenuous business of the afternoon that I realised what was meant by this altitude problem everyone was talking about. Although I smoke a good few cigarettes, I had never before in my life been short of wind. Now, after two or three sustained sprints, it suddenly became almost impossible to breathe, and I remember gasping desperately for relief. When my throat finally sucked in some elusive oxygen, its entry grated on the lungs like sandpaper – and I decided there and then that I had better leave for home on the next plane: hard as I had trained in preparation for the tour I was convinced that I could never, ever, play rugby properly under such conditions. Gareth Edwards, a Lion in 1968, assured me with a big grin that I would feel better before long; he got a big scowl (all I could manage!) for his pains.

It didn't help when I observed that Andy Ripley appeared in no distress at all and was gambolling around like a two-year-old.

Syd Millar, already familiar with the problems of adjusting to altitude, was sympathetic to those of us who were choking with oxygen starvation, but insisted that only by training hard and driving ourselves could we become accustomed to the thin air. So it was more pain and suffering for a whole week, relieved only by the helpful breathing exercises devised by our doctor-hooker Ken Kennedy. By the end of that time my lungs had just about learned how to draw in the sustenance they needed; but I still would have slept happily at my omission from the team for our first fixture against Western Transvaal had it not been for the fact that Andy Ripley won himself the first outing at number 8, and was able to figure in a 59-13 victory. Furthermore, it meant that I had to play in the second match against South-west Africa at Windhoek, a town which was 2000 feet higher still above sea-level! The last twenty minutes were again murder for tortured lungs, but we survived and won well by 23-16 after an encounter distinguished by some fine play from Jan Ellis, the Springbok flanker whom we well remembered from the 1970 tour in Britain.

Atmospheric pressures apart, in those first few days the British Isles once more demonstrated a healthy ability to sink national differences and become a happy, well-integrated unit. The generous hospitality of the host country helped the process, as did Choet Visser, our liaison officer, who whisked us smoothly between training sessions, receptions, barbecues, drinks parties and our hotels. A businessman, he had contacts the length and breadth of South Africa who could always fix Lions up with anything from a sight-seeing trip by car to a case of coke for quenching the thirst. Nor did his loyalty to the tourists waver except, understandably, during the days we spent preparing to meet (and beat) his home XV, Orange Free State.

Within the party strong personalities began to emerge as they had in New Zealand. Once he had recovered from a bout of tummy-trouble which beset him for a few days after our arrival, Bobby Windsor staked a claim as one of the prime wits of the tour. His instructions to waiters about how he liked his omelettes cooked were often laced with that dry humour that seems to be a speciality of men of Gwent. And I recall one breakfast-time when he asked a waitress, 'Could you bring me some cold coffee, then two hard fried eggs with brittle bacon and black fried bread, followed by two rounds of burned toast?' 'I don't think we could supply that kind of meal in this hotel,' came the affronted reply. 'Oh yes you could,' said Bobby. 'You served it yesterday.'

His inviting surname, of course, was prefixed with the nick-name 'Duke'. Mike Burton became known as 'Batman', either because he spent a lot of time up in the air during scrummaging practice or because he once mistook a hotel window for the door and found himself in mid-air ten feet off the ground – I am not sure which. Gareth Edward's relentless clowning earned him the nick-name 'Coco', while one player was dubbed 'Bungalow' because he apparently had nothing up top! I shall spare his blushes.

Amidst all the banter, however, Syd Millar was busy conditioning his men for their principal task on tour, to win the Test series. The first message he got across to us was that we were going to hit the Springboks at forward harder than they had ever been hit before in nearly a century's rugby football. What was more, as a sterling prop who had taken part in scores of hard matches for Ireland and the British Isles, Syd knew exactly how we were going to do it.

His whole idea was based on our suspicion that South African scrummaging, for long the cardinal virtue of their game, was on the wane – and this impression was confirmed as we pushed provincial packs all over the park in our first few games. Therefore we were going to spend a lot of time and effort perfecting our own packing and shoving. If we could become good enough to cause a Springbok eight to give ground, it would deal our opponents a devastating physical and psychological blow besides raising our own morale immeasurably.

Thus at practice Millar, quite the most single-minded coach I ever worked under, gave us scrummaging, scrummaging and still more scrummaging. Later on it was to become tedious, but I have to admit that at first it produced precisely the required result. Syd reversed the idea treasured by many forwards that a set scrum is a place where you can afford to lean on your opponents and take a quick, surreptitious breather: the 1974 Lions quickly learned that it was one where your work-rate went up, not down.

Such a preoccupation meant that the coach spent more time with the forwards than with the backs. But I don't think this caused us to lose any sleep, for we knew that behind the forwards we had a talented bunch of men, quite capable of playing together well and devising their own winning moves. As far as I was concerned, so long as the backs put to good use the possession we won for them and demonstrated that they were organised, which they did, then I was happy. In many games, as it turned out, our pack's superiority guaranteed us the victory, but when this was not the case the backs came to the rescue and saw us through.

For training, incidentally, the Lions had each been asked to include in their baggage one red and one white jersey. This is something I recommend to all club squads, since it brings undoubted clarity to practice sessions, especially when unopposed or touch rugby is being played. Mind you, the Irish way of playing 'touch' rugby, as conceived by Millar and McBride, turned out to be rather more violent than we in Wales are used to!

By the end of May I had three provincial appearances under my belt, plus a feeling that my game was reapproaching its normal standard. But that man Ripley's play in the other matches had earned my respect, and I conceded to myself that this superb athlete was a great runner with the ball. If his distribution lacked finesse, he made up for it with great enthusiasm and drive. His performances were certainly fuelling my renewed endeavour, prompting me to tell myself, 'Merv, you've got a fight on your hands, but there's no way Andy's going to oust you from the Test side.' Privately I considered that his knowledge of the modern number 8 game was less than complete, but I was taking nothing for granted.

So I was on tenterhooks when the thirty of us gathered at our Cape Town hotel to hear the team chosen to play in the first Test on 8 June. By now the Lions had seven convincing wins to their credit, to which practically every member of the party had contributed, and it was felt that all fifteen places were wide open to all of us, save poor Tom David and Roy Bergiers, prevented by injury from mounting a sustained challenge for selection.

As Syd went through the list some men looked content, the faces of others fell a little. But since the number 8 is the last position of the lot to be announced I had to sit impatiently while fourteen names were read out before hearing my own. Although he must have been sorely disappointed, Andy, with whom I have always enjoyed a most cordial relationship on and off the field, was the first to congratulate me. I had, then, weathered a personal crisis: could we now, as a team, come out on top?

The selected side was certainly the strongest available, and the only major casualty had been the England stand-off half Alan Old, known to us as 'E.N.T.' because he had big ears, a big nose, and talked a lot! From the time we first sank a pint or two together back at the London hotel, I had enjoyed the company of this down-to-earth Yorkshireman, whose 37 points during our 97-0 win over South Western Districts were the most by any touring player in a match in South Africa. So I was desperately sorry when a severe injury sustained against the Proteas in Cape Town put him into hospital and out of the tour. Phil Bennett was, too, even though Alan's absence provided him with a clear entrance into the Test side.

Few of the chosen South African XV were well known to us. I have spoken of Jan Ellis as an old-established opponent, while the veteran Hannes Marais had been recalled to captain the side from prop. Otherwise, we noticed, the Springboks included seven players from the Western Province side which had given us a tough game a week earlier. That was a first clue to something which became crystal clear as the series progressed: uncertain of their judgement, South Africa's selectors were prepared to clutch at straws rather than graft away at the business of welding a strong team.

For once the weather and the conditions seemed to favour the tourists, for the Saturday morning in Cape Town dawned grey and drizzle-soaked. Early reports suggested that the Test pitch would be a quagmire, and this was made certain by the reckless playing of two junior games on it in the morning. However, there was no complacency in our camp, and the silence before Willie John delivered his 11 am pep-talk was electric. His words were inspiring, but perhaps I remember more vividly the few terse sentences gritted out by our coach. 'We shall go forward,' Millar rasped. 'We shall go on. We shall overcome.' And then, emphasising the ruthlessness of the approach he wanted, 'We shall take no prisoners.'

If Andy Ripley had helped to revive my game, the supreme thrill of Test match rugby put the final polish on it. I proved the point in the first clash with South Africa by bringing off the most satisfying tackle I have ever made in my career. The 'Boks' flanker Boland Coetzee was my victim, and as he supported a narrow side break by his wing and was receiving the inside pass I drove into him just below the ribs. His breath exhaled with a noise somewhere between a grunt and a moan and his body jerked back two or three metres. We won the ruck, the crowd groaned, and I knew that I had gone a long way towards establishing ascendancy over South Africa's back row.

Elsewhere, other Lions were busy making similar points, for we had taken the field knowing that it was ultra-important to win this first game and get our noses ahead in the rubber. As it turned out we failed to score a try (though I came close to glory after charging down a clearance attempt by du Plessis) but the three penalties by Phil Bennett and a big dropped goal by Gareth Edwards against just one penalty for South Africa fairly reflected our territorial dominance and superiority in all aspects of the play. The non-stop aggression of Bobby Windsor, who had played himself into the Test side ahead of the experienced Kennedy, was typical of an eight which did, as we had planned, out-scrummage the opposition.

And as a matter of fact, my own chief reaction to the result was one of disappointment that the alleged giants of world rugby had failed to respond with nobility to the challenge we mounted that day. Furthermore, since the muddy surface had prevented us from developing a running game, I felt that the outlook for the Springboks was doubly ominous: they had yet to experience the best that the Lions could produce.

The South Africans appeared to take their defeat well, and at the post-match dinner we attributed quietness on their part to the language barrier: for many of them, Afrikaans was the first language, and communication in English not always easy. Their captain, Hannes Marais, delivered a complimentary and perfectly adequate speech which confirmed my impression of him as a nice guy — though perhaps too nice to crack the whip and be a stern task-master of his team.

But out and about the city the home supporters seemed as shell-shocked as New Zealand folk had been three years before. Perhaps the disappointment they felt was even more bitter, for their relative isolation in world sport seemed to have bred a particularly fervent and demonstrative type of nationalism, which manifested itself in utter loyalty to their International players. Nonetheless nothing but magnanimous praise was accorded to their visitors for their achievement.

During our visit to Cape Town we paid an eye-opening visit to the great rugby hot-bed of Stellenbosch University where Dr Danie Craven, then Head of its Faculty of Physical Education, had built up an incredible complex of facilities. Besides a dozen or so rugby pitches we noted his legendary 'assault course' consisting of undulating sandy tracks through a sprawling tangle of undergrowth, which makes Ray Prosser's Pontypool set-up seem like a children's playground, not to mention piles of boulders and logs which, we were told, budding locks and props had to hump around to improve their strength and endeavour. Truly this was a finishing-school of rugby football.

After we had held a training session (in which I studiously avoided logs and rocks) Dr Craven entertained us to drinks. This meeting with 'Mr Rugby' broke down the preconceived idea I had of him as a cold, inflexible and rather one-eyed theorist on the game. He talked to us easily and agreeably and it was flattering to find that, far from being dogmatic and authoritarian, he actually seemed interested in the ideas advanced by us young Lions. I doubt whether I shall be able to reproduce his boyish enthusiasm for everything to do with rugby football when I reach the age of sixty-three.

We defeated Southern Universities and Transvaal before flying up to Salisbury to give Rhodesia a beating by 42 points to 6. It was there that news reached us of the eight changes South Africa's selectors had made for the second Test at Pretoria (they were to use thirty-three players altogether in the series, which prompted Dr Craven's remark that they had run out of green serge for blazers, which are awarded to Springboks instead of caps). Eight changes! We could scarcely believe our ears. But we must be on to a good thing, for the opposition was obviously at panic stations.

In spite of the confidence with which we took the field, the result of the Test still exceeded our highest expectations. Once more we quickly established domination up front, so that although at one time our lead was a bare 10-6 we ultimately galloped away to inflict upon South Africa her heaviest defeat in International football, by 28 points to 9.

It was especially pleasing to have produced such a crushing retort to critics (not all of them South African) who were accusing us of playing boring, ten-man rugby. That day the backs came into their own, proved that they were not there simply to make up the numbers, and scored all but three of our points. For the record, J. J. Williams got two tries, and Brown, Milliken and Bennett one each, while the latter also kicked a penalty and a conversion. Ian McGeechan dropped a goal.

'They haven't got an answer to us, Swerve,' said my back-row partners Fergus Slattery and Roger Uttley as we jubilantly downed pints of fruit juice and coke in the changing-room afterwards. Although we hadn't contributed to the big score-line we had worked splendidly as a trio, with Roger and myself playing as tight forwards and Slats shooting off to hunt the halves and midfield backs at high speed. What a competitor the Irishman was: if he didn't nail the opposing stand-off half three or four times during a game he considered that he had had a poor afternoon's sport!

So the Lions were two-up in the series and could not now be defeated. A great position to have gained — and we thought we deserved a few days off!

Kruger Park turned out to be our half-way house this time, a game reserve that is bigger than the whole of Wales. We were put up in a holiday camp where the accommodation consisted of mud huts which all looked alike, so that after dark and a number of jugs of ale many of the boys had considerable difficulty in finding their way home. Sometimes the South African night would prove unnerving, for wild boars would occasionally penetrate the camp area, and every now and then a hippopotamus would startle us by bellowing in a nearby river. 'Batman' Burton and Stew McKinney also devised a way of amusing themselves which consisted of leaping from trees with wild cries and putting the wind up more timid Lions. We told them that had we not been in a game reserve they would have been gunned down without mercy.

Dawn and dusk expeditions (I settled for the latter) took us to view the real wild animals, at water-holes about an hour's drive into the bush. We saw lions, giraffe, wildebeest, and of course springboks, at whose smallness I was quite surprised. But then, perhaps that was how their human counterparts were feeling at that moment.

The only trouble with Kruger Park was that no alcohol is sold within it, so that although the Lions had imported gallons of the stuff we got through it even more quickly than manager Alun Thomas had anticipated. For the final forty-eight hours we went without even a single glassful of beer, and experienced the kind of thirst that I suppose was common in Wales when Sundays were dry.

Any feeling of over-confidence or relaxation which threatened to creep in during our stay in the park was soon dashed when we took a long look at the fixtures which confronted us in the fortnight before we met South Africa in the third Test. The Quaggas, the local equivalent of the Barbarians, a powerful Orange Free State XV and Northern Transvaal all looked like posing major threats to our proud hundred-per-cent record.

It crossed my mind, though, as we travelled towards Johannesburg and the Quaggas encounter, that I had seldom felt healthier in my life. Oxygen starvation was now a thing of the past, and the sharp, clean air brushed cobwebs straight out of the system as I awoke each day. Our diet was magnificent: if we felt so inclined we could eat steak for breakfast, lunch and dinner. Lots of sunshine had turned most of us a glamorous shade of brown.

At this stage we were also thoroughly used to South African pitches, which, except on the coast, are harder and more arid then ours in Britain. The Lions' medical trunk at the outset of the tour was loaded with ointments and wrappings for joints which might be vulnerable to the notorious 'grass burns' which had created serious problems for our predecessors. Now, however, only Gordon Brown continued to protect his knees with bandage, and most of us were confident that our limbs had toughened themselves sufficiently to withstand the grazes which afflict tender skins when you first go to ground on the veld. We had also learned that short studs were the answer if one wished to avoid painful blisters when running over the brown-stained, sun-baked South African turf. Andy Ripley was the only blister victim I can recall, and maybe his trouble stemmed from the fact that, as a super-casual dresser, he wore sandals throughout the tour.

Our place-kickers, Phil Bennett and Andy Irvine, had spurned the use of the sand-box brought out during matches to assist in teeing-up the ball. The Springbok experts tended to be toe-kickers, whose technique demanded careful propping of the ball, but Phil and Andy, 'round-the-corner' men, found there was just enough give in the grass to make their more simple placement possible.

So, as a team, we had few worries. Pocket money, since raised to £2.50, was then still a meagre 75p a day, but because of our hosts' enormous generosity we rarely had to put our hands into our pockets. I had also been extremely generously treated by my new employers, the Blyth firm of Swansea, who had kept me on full salary during the tour. There was sympathy, though, for teacher colleagues like Roy Bergiers and J. J. Williams whose education authorities in South Wales had declined to pay them while away from their jobs. It seemed crazy to me that great athletes should suffer because of the whims of a few administrators, especially as a trip such as we were on could not help but broaden the mind and experience of every tourist and give him an immense amount to contribute on his return.

We had also managed to avoid the bad publicity which followed the 1968 British Lions around, when a succession of South African hotels reported horse-play which resulted in damage and breakages that went beyond the bounds of common sense. I can only repeat my view that the watershed had been surmounted by 1974, and that my contemporaries and I were a different breed of tourists. And talking of dedication, none showed more than Andy Ripley, whose total commitment always prompted me never to slacken efforts to hold my Test place.

Our expectation that the Quaggas XV would comprise young,

uncapped Springbok Test hopefuls proved wide of the mark when they fielded a side that contained four full International players. Although we were given a hard contest and scored three tries to their one, the result was a close 20-16 win. Two days later at Bloemfontein only a remarkable last-gasp try executed by Gareth Edwards and J. J. Williams saved us from defeat: the two Welshmen performed an impromptu scissors move to get the score after Bobby Windsor had won a strike against the head on the Orange Free State line. This was certainly the 1974 Lions' narrowest escape from defeat, and I was glad to have contributed an early try (one of five I obtained in all) through stretching my long frame to the line after a short burst off the base of a set scrum. Again, a week later in Pretoria, we had to hit top form to beat Northern Transvaal 16-12.

Such games brought the rested Lions back to concert pitch, but I must make the point that interspersed with hard outings there were always fixtures in which we found no trouble in running up 50, 60 or more points, such as those with the South African 'Africans' – the Leopards – Griqualand West and South Western Districts. This bears out a view which I have expressed before, that a South African tour is not as demanding week-in week-out as one in New Zealand. In my experience the latter country offers no matches at all in which weary tourists can relax a little. ·

It was a wonderful feeling, though, to enter the third Test with the knowledge that the rubber was ours if we won or drew. Our pre-match confidence was again inflated by the astonishing fickleness of the Springbok selectors. This time they had made no fewer than eleven changes and dropped the giant John G. Williams, who was in our opinion a world-class line-out forward. I must say that this lack of faith reminded me of the English selectors back home; it is impossible to forge a top-grade rugby team unless you are prepared to let the players settle down and cohere into a unit. A reverse or two may have to be suffered, but a certain amount of perseverance is preferable to total panic. Eleven changes! Words fail me.

This overall crisis of confidence was reflected most vividly in that sector of the conflict where I was most keenly engaged, the forward struggle. By the time the third Test came along our opponents might have been expected to settle upon an eight who could at least seek parity with the Lions. Instead their forwards were yet again a ragged bunch of men, who had no chance of performing well against a Lions pack that was unchanged for a third time running.

Thus the momentum they generated was about as effective as an aerosol spray. Their rucking and mauling was completely disjointed, and at the set scrummages we could hear Marais and his locks squabbling about basic technique such as where feet were to be planted and by what route the ball was to be channelled back to poor Sonnekus at scrum-half. My own opposite number that day, incidentally, was Kritzinger, who had the doubtful privilege of succeeding Morne du Plessis and Dugald MacDonald; and when he in turn was subsequently axed in favour of Grobler, it gave me the personal distinction of having played four number 8 forwards out of Test reckoning – five if we count Ripley!

John J. Williams got another brace of tries to establish a Test series record, and Gordon Brown scored a third, while Irvine and Bennett notched 14 points between them with a variety of kicks. South Africa's only replies were three penalties by Snyman, so that we had romped to another sensational victory by 26 points to 9. We had won the series, and it was third time lucky for our captain Willie John McBride after his two dreary experiences in 1962 and 1968. Another of rugby's memorable, nay unforgettable, days.

It is worth recalling that South Africa had tried to disrupt our game that day by an over-physical approach. This was the time when we had recourse to our famous '99' call, which meant that oblivious to the consequences all eight forwards got stuck into their opposite numbers if there was provocation, and hotted things up for a few moments. It may have been illegal, but there was nothing practicable that the referee could do about such collective action, and it served our purpose: it showed that this particular generation of Britons was not to be trifled with. My sole regret after the two incidents of this nature in the Test was that, following what he later described as the 'altercations', our Scottish lock Gordon Brown hurt a hand and could not be considered for the fourth match. Still, it meant that Chris Ralston was to get a game which lifted him for eighty minutes from among the ranks of the 'dirt-trackers', the pet name for our Wednesday XV.

Little of importance disturbed our happy progress as the tour drew towards its close, except a bruising game against Natal in which John P. R. Williams and local hero Tommy Bedford had their celebrated punch-up. I am not going to exonerate John from blame, of which he must bear fifty per cent, but I took a dim view of the crowd's showering us with empty beer cans, which could have caused serious injury. Still, I could understand their chagrin at Natal's spanking defeat by 34 points to 6. Four of the points came from my last try of the tour.

As in New Zealand, so this time the fourth Test ended in a draw. However, in 1974 we felt disappointment rather than delight at the 13-13 score-line, since our hopes of white-washing the Springboks and taking home an unsurpassable tour record of twenty-two wins out of twenty-two games had been thwarted. South Africa's total included their solitary try of the rubber against us, scored by Cronje, while we had registered touch-downs through Uttley and Irvine. In the dying moments Fergus Slattery scored what he later said was a perfectly good try which would have given us the spoils. I agreed with him, having been a bare 5 metres distant, but Max Baise disallowed it — and that was that.

Nonetheless Johannesburg was a tremendous climax to a wonderful tour, and yet again a Lions side in which I had played a significant role could claim to have made history. A crowd of 75,000 had paid a record £300,000 to see the Unbeaten Lions' final performance beneath the towering stands and terraces of Ellis Park, and perhaps the finest compliment those supporters could have paid us was their chairing from the field of the Springbok captain Hannes Marais after the final whistle: a skipper whose achievement was to inspire his team to avoid a fourth successive defeat!

Although no British Isles side this century had approached our record there was still the inevitable sniping from critics who said that South Africa's rugby had gone back a long way and that in 1974 they were easy meat. Two years later, viewed on celluloid on the big screen at a charity film night in a South Wales club, the Test matches didn't show the Springboks in that bad a light. And having been tops for seventy-five years, how on earth could they suddenly become so very bad at the game? Why didn't such critics, I asked myself wryly, simply settle for the fact that the Lions had been an outstanding side? Anyway, as I have remarked before, you tend to dismiss carping and denigration from your mind when, in the last analysis, you can say: 'The Lions $3\frac{1}{2}$, South Africa $\frac{1}{2}$.'

I have two final comments to make, one of which is on apartheid. I shall say no more than this: at our matches I noticed that while Whites were comfortably seated, often in the shade, Blacks had to stand on the terrace at one end of the ground, usually that facing into the sun. This, plus Black support for the Lions and evident hostility for South Africa's 'representatives' on the field, led me to draw my own conclusions about the validity of the apartheid policy. Further than that, bearing in mind my own principle that sport and politics should not be mixed, I am not prepared to go.

Second, to the question I am so often asked: 'Which was the better Lions XV, that of 1971 or that of 1974?' I usually reply that if the 1971 backs could have been teamed with the 1974 pack, the outcome would have been a combination capable of matching any team fielded this century. That is the diplomatic answer!

However, if you press me on such an imponderable topic, I shall have to concede that the quality of the opposition encountered in New Zealand constituted a sterner, more consistent challenge than that which we overcame in South Africa. Only on this basis can I separate two great British Isles touring parties and conclude that the 1971 achievement narrowly takes the palm.

Really, though, both tours should be viewed together as proof that in the first half of the 1970s British rugby was, for a change, the best in the world. A testimony to which I shall always be grateful to have contributed.

8   *Number 8s are not Donkeys*

David Parry-Jones

For most of the nineteen-sixties Alun Pask, a tall and agile product of Abertillery RFC, was the prime exponent of number 8 forward play. The winner of twenty-six Welsh caps, he was deferred to both in the United Kingdom and far beyond, and when he participated in their 1964 centenary games the South Africans described him as the world's best player in his position.

Certainly the sight of the big fellow on the move through midfield, surging along with the ball often brandished like a melon in one enormous fist, delighted the crowds. His hands were good, his pace impressive, and in the days before replacements were allowed he could stand in for an injured team-mate anywhere between full-back and second row. Pask was not noted for his contribution to what was then broadly termed 'loose' forward play, but in his defence it should be remembered that in Wales the tactical possibilities of expert rucking and mauling had yet to be appreciated fully.

There was, thus, a tremendous contrast between the Abertillery man and the next number 8 to establish himself in the Welsh XV, as great aesthetically and practically as that between a snorting shire-horse, flush with nervous energy, and a large, phlegmatic, grizzly bear. For Mervyn Davies will not be recalled as a speed-merchant in the open field, forever side-stepping or accelerating his way past bewildered, wrong-footed opponents. He was not a scorer of spectacular, glamorous tries, who hurled himself in at the corner flag after sprinting clear from 25 metres' range. Indeed, having been conditioned to the Pask style of play during seven seasons at International level, it took Welsh crowds at least two years to appreciate to the full the different range of virtues possessed by the London Welshman.

And even then only gradually did it dawn on observers and critics how deliberately and with what sure purpose Merv applied his strengths to the pressure points of rugby football. For people first had to grasp the new importance of ruck and maul, as highlighted by those who were seeking to revolutionise the Welsh game; only then could they discern the skill and expertise with which the newcomer transformed loose situations into sturdy plat-forms for winning the second phase. The swift turning of opponents to render the ball vulnerable to predatory team-mates, the ability to bind an eight together and drive through the ruck while remaining upright, the application of outsize shoulders, elbows and hands to acts of robbery perpetrated at the heart of the maul — these were crafts brought to a very high degree of excellence. And because they had been practised by relatively few predecessors they did not im-mediately win the accolade accorded to them in later years.

It goes almost without saying that Mervyn Davies's execution of rugby football's basic techniques was of a very high order. It took an outstandingly nimble opponent to defeat his tackle in a one-to-one confrontation. He rarely mishandled, while fellow forwards testify to the effort he put into set-pieces. At the beginning of his career, as one of the tallest players in Britain, he founded a reputa-tion for consistently competitive and accurate line-out jumping, nor was he ever guilty of the badly directed taps and flaps which so alarm and dismay scrum-halves. In short, he was a number 8 forward who played, by preference, a tight, meticulous sort of game, and whose all round skill could scarcely be faulted.

There is one other point to make, concerning his sense of an-ticipation. He himself finds difficulty in rationalising its origins, and is inclined to put it down mainly to experience. But anyone who takes the trouble to browse through the thousands of action photographs in which he figures cannot fail to be struck by one feature they have in common: where Mervyn is not actually the ball-carrier it is astonishing to note how regularly and consistently he appears in very close attendance. Whether it is a wing or a stand-off half or an enterprising full-back who is spear-heading the attack, the tall man with the head-band is seldom more than 6 or 8 metres distant, picking up speed, hands at the ready, mouth occasionally open as he shouts a message of support to his team-mate.

On reflection, perhaps the pictorial evidence is the most important monument of all to Mervyn Davies's greatness. All his fans will retain in the memory privately-treasured images of him in action – leaping like a salmon at the end of a line-out, ripping clean ball away from the fringe of a maul, or clobbering a stand-off half who thought he was through the gap. These were moments which caused the terraces to seethe with excitement and brought deep-throated bayings of approval from fifty thousand admirers.

The pictures preserve a facet of his game which the crowds seldom noticed. They document him as a number 8 whose pace never flagged, as an eighty-minute player who was never far from the eye of the storm.

MERVYN DAVIES

Commercial representatives are, on the whole, a methodical breed of men, most of whom map out each day's schedule well in advance. My own approach to my job is, I have to admit, rather different.

I am the sort of person who wakes up in the morning, scratches his head, decides what day it is, and only then, over a pre-breakfast cuppa, asks himself, 'Whom shall I call on today?' which means that some industrialist or other gets a coffee-time surprise when Mr Mervyn Davies presents his compliments out of the blue and requests the pleasure of a business conversation. I don't often get sent packing, for even captains of industry enjoy a break from desk-work to gossip about rugby matters of moment in Wales, and I cannot complain about the number of orders which come my way, but that's not the point. For me a flexible life-style is a 'must' and I would chafe at any kind of set routine. I cherish my freedom.

That is, I am sure, the principal reason why I have derived so much pleasure from playing the whole of my rugby life-span in the number 8 position. It is, you see, one where the rules are few, and certainly no manual exists which the beginner can pick up and follow. At number 8 you have to make your own way and seek your own destiny, relying at first on common sense and instinct and later on carefully hoarded experience. The theme song for a recently retired number 8 could well be 'I did it my way' – for there is no other. At the same time one can assert proudly that the position does allow a man to give expression to all the skills and stratagems that rugby football has to offer.

The trouble is that this heady freedom sets me a knotty problem in trying to define what should be the role of the number 8 on the field. If I were asked to set down what should be expected of a lock like Geoff Wheel, front-row men like Bobby Windsor or Charlie Faulkner, or flankers like Trevor Evans and Terry Cobner, I should be able to make a fair attempt. During eight years in the first-class game it became a straightforward matter to decide when they were playing to maximum effect and what was going wrong if they were not.

Nor would I be at a loss if asked to sum up the contributions that can be made by, say, full-backs or scrum-halves. I could point out that John P. R. Williams does the basics well, such as tackling and kicking to touch, and that his greatness derives from the superb in-itiative he demonstrates when running out of defence or entering the line. I should comment that while Gareth Edwards is primarily a feeder of the backs he puts opposing defences into a turmoil with brilliant breaks from scrum or line-out. And though I don't hand out many compliments to backs, I would even be prepared to admit that when the chips are down he can be as useful as a fourth back-row forward!

Believe me, I find it far harder to discuss my own position. However, since I truly consider it to be the most important one in the team (whatever Barry John or Phil Bennett might suggest!), I shall make the attempt to describe the options that are open to its occupier. And there are many: you have only to compare the widely differing styles of play of, say, Andy Ripley, Tommy Bedford and myself to appreciate that the man in the middle of the back row can select an approach to the game that suits him best. So, if you are a budding number 8 forward who expects me to assert, 'You must do it this way,' then you will be disappointed.

For I can declare that no previous holder of the position influenc-ed my play in any way, nor did I set out to model my game on anyone else's. But there was a good reason for this, namely evolution within rugby itself. When I was a youngster people still referred to the number 8 as a 'lock' (we imported the modern term from South Africa, whose second-row men were always known as locks). Since halves and three-quarters, and flankers too, commonly lay up close on the opposition, the 'lock' distinguished himself in defence by 'corner-flagging'; that is to say, following a course towards the corner-flag towards which the attacking backs were running. The idea, as I understand it, was to pick up kicks ahead or to cut off an opposing wing who had avoided a tackle. All very clever: but I suspect that in practice things seldom worked out that way, for it must have meant that the 'lock' effectively became a non-participant in loose play. As for covering, if you are heading full-tilt in one direction it is just too easy to be beaten by an inside jink on the part of the man you are supposed to be stalking.

In 1968, however, changes in the off-side law, particularly at the line-out, obliged the two sets of backs to stand some 20 metres apart. Immediately there was created an empty sector of the field behind the line-out, into which the flow of support players in attack and defence became a prime need the moment the set-piece had ended. At one stroke this rendered 'corner-flagging' obsolete. Hence my generation of number 8 forwards has been the first to leave set-pieces in a cross-field, or preferably up-field, direction, as opposed to consistently retreating away from the action. This change of emphasis has a bearing on part of what I have to say, and certainly governed a great deal of my own movements in open play.

Next, then, let us consider what manner of man makes an ideal number 8 forward in the modern game. These days he needs to be at least 6 feet 3 inches in order to be able to compete effectively at the tail of the line-out. He ought to turn the scales at between $14\frac{1}{2}$ and 16 stones: that is, he must be heavy enough to contribute adequately to a scrummage drive, but not so ponderous that he will be slow around the field or leaden-footed when jumping for the ball.

He will have to be a very dedicated sort of fellow, for in my experience he will need to be the fittest man on the field, with great reserves of stamina. The rhythm and momentum of his game differ considerably from the way most of his colleagues must play. For example, backs spend perhaps twenty per cent of their game in dynamic bursts of activity, and the rest of the time adjusting and readjusting their positions without expending too much energy. Props and locks use up huge amounts of upper-body strength shoving, tugging and wrestling at scrummages and mauls for, say, fifty per cent of the time and have what amounts to a licence to husband their resources as they move from one such situation to the next. But the number 8 forward can never slow down or ease up: he is required to exert at least seventy-five per cent of his strength and speed for the whole of the eighty minutes.

This is no idle statement, since his role is two-fold. He must be prepared for action as a scrummaging forward, which means shoving hard and combining as a member of what I like to call the 'tight six' (I think that the term 'front five' is a misnomer). Second, he must be able to move quickly from set-pieces to help repossess the ball from the second phase in attack or defence, to execute a straightforward tackle, or to lend support to a handling movement.

So before we get too technical, let us pause to see how a number 8 prepares himself for such an all-round performance. Which brings me to that painful subject, training.

Now, there are two stages of training: the first usually comes before or at the start of a new season, and involves the slow, sometimes agonising build-up of stamina and endurance. This was the only part of the whole rugby scene which I must admit to having found utterly boring, and as my career progressed to maturity I was not the most regular and ever-present attender of practice sessions. Quite often at Swansea big Barry Clegg or one of the other jokers would greet me on Saturday afternoons with a terse 'Must have been a bad attack of dandruff you had last Tuesday evening, Merv!'

The point is that I was lucky enough to be one of those types who don't have to train frantically to stay fit. Some players, like Derek Quinnell, Roger Blyth, and even Phil Bennett, have only to look at a cream cake to put on extra poundage; in contrast, far from having problems, I actually used to shed weight in the summer, replacing it in the winter as the odd roll of fat hardened again into muscle. I was never short of wind, and my limbs always seemed to be good and supple.

13. The clean catch at a line-out is a valuable but sadly neglected skill these days. Tommy Bedford of Natal can only watch while the 1974 Lions decide how to use the possession won by Mervyn

14. Hail the conquering hero: Reunited with Shirley, Mervyn comes home to Pontlliw after the unbeaten Lions' tour of South Africa in 1974

15. A Lion in the family—with proud parents Betty and Dai, and wife Shirley. Merv looks slightly shell-shocked from the warmth of his welcome back to Wales!

16. Parc des Princes, 1975—Mervyn Davies's first match as captain of Wales. But the skipper was tormented by doubts

17. Nevertheless he inspired his team, containing six new caps, to victory by 25-10 —and the critics had to eat their words

18. At a line-out the number 8 forward can be the provider of precious quality possession for his team

19. Huge totals scored by Wales on their Far Eastern Tour of 1975 showed the Japanese where they stood in the game. Here Mervyn scores in Tokyo despite the attentions of Ogasawara (left), Japan's outstanding forward of recent years

20. *The Swansea club fully understood Mervyn's feelings about the pressures experienced by top players like himself and Geoff Wheel. But here the two star All Whites seem destined to be robbed by a Barbarian at St Helen's in 1975*

21. *Mervyn leads out the Barbarians to play the traditional end-of-tour match against the Wallabies at Cardiff in January 1976. But sometimes he declined invitations to play for the Baa-Baas*

22. (above) *Mervyn cleans up untidy possession in his last International match for Wales, the Grand Slam clincher in 1976. Gareth Edwards waits: 'Gareth and I brought communication between number 8 and scrum-half to a fine art'*

23. (right) *Patient of the Year!—Merv and one of the 4000 greeting cards he received while at the University of Wales hospital in Cardiff. The staff found him, if not quite a model patient, a co-operative one!*

24. (right) *Merv, Morecambe and Wise at Buckingham Palace to receive OBEs. The investiture audience tittered when the comedians met the Queen*

25. (below) *Mervyn and his great New Zealand rival, lock forward Colin Meads, who flew 12,000 miles for his brief appearance on* This is Your Life. *Mervyn returns the compliment by including Meads in his World XV*

Nowadays I occasionally reflect that had I donned spikes or taken up weight training I might have been an even better player; but during my career it seldom occurred to me that extra physical exertion could do much to improve my basic ability.

So I was an exception to the rule. My advice to young number 8 forwards, though, is to drive yourselves like demons so that you can achieve everything within a match that you set out to do. And although you will have gathered that I did not train with enormous enthusiasm, let me emphasise that I was never a quitter: during a fitness session I gave everything that I had and invariably stayed in harness until the bitter end.

That, then, is the hard grind of getting and staying fit – stage one. Once the second stage of training had been reached, and a ball was introduced for the practice of skills, Merv the Swerve really came to life. In a straightforward 50-metre sprint I might finish last, but if a ball was kicked ahead of the squad and fifteen of us were told to hare after it I would always be among the first two or three in the race. Surely there is a moral here for all coaches planning their squad training.

Talking of coaches, it often amused me to see if I could steal a march on them. On the 1971 Lions tour Carwyn James would sometimes snap out, 'Everybody in pairs! Give your partners piggy-back rides as far as the half-way line!' I would loiter a few yards away until the other fourteen had paired off before affecting dismay that I had somehow got left out. The trouble all too often was that a cheery Scottish voice would call from behind me, 'OK, Merv – you can carry me!' There would be the huge shape of Doug Smith waiting for a lift.

The only Lion who got away with murder at training was Barry John. A great player, I suppose, can be a law unto himself, but the rest of us honest toilers would feel rather hard-done-by when he would murmur, 'The old back is a bit stiff today, Carwyn.' Our coach would nod, and off sloped the 'King'. Within five minutes he could be observed keeping goal in some impromptu soccer match with the reserve XV, when his spectacular dives to turn the ball around a post suggested that there was not a lot wrong with his lumbar region! However, his team-mates would be quick to forgive

F

Gren's cartoon solves the mystery of Merv's head-band

him when he won the following Saturday's match for us with a solo try or a couple of long-range penalties.

My final word on this topic is that, although they can assist and stimulate players' drive to attain fitness, club coaches have a right to expect that their men are in good fettle by the time squad practice begins in earnest. This is especially true at national level, where the coach needs all the time available to plot the course of the game and the tactics to be employed. Rugby football is a team game, but one in which individuals must accept responsibility to prepare themselves thoroughly for participation in it.

Before we return to discuss match play, there are one or two things worth saying about preparing for a game in the changing-room. People often ask about the broad white head-band which was my trade-mark on the pitch, and which once led a Welsh cartoonist to suggest that it hid my lack of ears (see above)!

I took to binding my head at a relatively early age on the advice of my father. As a former lock or second-row forward, Dai Davies knew all about the severe pressures ears are subjected to as the hip bones of players in front lock together at a scrummage and grind

upon one's temples. 'I don't think you can avoid getting a cauliflower ear or two, Mervyn,' he warned me, 'but wearing a head-band will cut down the pain a bit.' He was right: I have got a 'cauli' (though it isn't as flamboyant as the two owned by Alun Pask!), but his tip did save me a lot of discomfort, and other modern forwards like Ian McLauchlan, Alan Martin and Garrick Fay have sensibly followed suit. J. P. R. Williams does not qualify for membership of this exclusive club, since his bandage was more of a hair-net to control his flowing locks!

The Irishmen Ray McLoughlin and Dennis Hickie are the only contemporaries I can recall who donned the more traditional scrum cap, which I decided against because it is cumbersome and because, being tied beneath the chin, it could choke the wearer if tugged from behind by an opponent.

Thinking back, the condition of my head-band at the end of a game was a personal yard-stick for assessing how well I had played. If it could be detached easily from my hair, the reason was that the adhesive had been diluted by perspiration – therefore I had been expending some energy. If it was dry and still tightly stuck, then I couldn't have had a very busy afternoon.

So I commend head-bands to scrummaging forwards, as well as other legal protective devices available to rugby players. You will recall how I had a tooth knocked out early in my career: not long after that, closing the stable door after one horse had bolted, I began using a gum-shield. This I particularly recommend, for it not only protects the teeth but is also capable of cushioning severe blows to the jaw such as inevitably come one's way from time to time in a maul or when taking a hard tackle. After a while I wondered how on earth I had managed without one, and if you ever saw me break off in the early stages of a game to consult a touch-judge or first-aid man urgently, it was probably because that gum-shield had been forgotten and I wanted it fetched from the changing-room.

For certain pitches, notably in South Africa, I wore a knee bandage, while in the early seventies, when the law still permitted scrum-halves to kick the ball out of the opposing back row, I bound my ankles to save them from unnecessary cuts and bruising, a habit I persevered with right to the end. Some players smother themselves in Vaseline in the hope of minimising grazes and scrapes, but I decided against doing so after finding that it rubbed off after about ten minutes' play, simply leaving the fingers sticky and liable to become coated with mud.

What with one thing and another, though, Merv the Swerve usually took the field in a well-armoured state. Once there, how can a number 8 set out to apply his power effectively and influence the play?

To take the set scrum first. The angle of shove for props and locks is an unnatural one, varying between 90° and about 120°. It is possible for the number 8, however, to stretch himself out to almost 180°, which is relatively quite comfortable. Therefore he must spare no effort to assist with the 'snap-shove', a movement designed to shift the set-piece forward by six inches or so. This is perfectly sufficient either to win the ball on one's own head or to slow down the opposition's heel. Arm and shoulder strength must also be applied to knit or 'lock' the scrummage in order to concentrate the shove.

If his hooker's strike is successful, a low, well-balanced shoving position allows the number 8 to use one foot to control and channel possession. He can hold the ball, swoop for a fast pick-up or, most often, release it at the right moment and in the best position for his scrum-half.

Communication between these two players is all-important, and I like to think that for Wales and the Lions Gareth Edwards and I brought it to a fine art. *'Gâd hi miwn!'* Gareth would bark, *'Wi'm yn moyn hi nawr!'* Or, *'Nawr! – fi i ti, ti i fi!'* These rapid-fire exchanges were usually in the Welsh language, which kept opponents guessing, and for which I had just enough vocabulary to get by. As a son of Welsh-speaking parents, incidentally, I regret that my command of the language is not better, and have not ruled out the idea of evening classes to improve it when there is time. I doubt, though, whether I could ever match the fluency of my garrulous friend from Gwaun-cae-Gurwen, who was made a Bard of the Royal National Eisteddfod in 1976.

The point is that, with the ball at his feet after a good heel, the number 8 can exercise considerable control of subsequent events if he is kept informed of the state of play behind the scrum. He can take pressure off a scrum-half who is being harassed by gathering the ball himself and driving forward close to the scrum, scattering the opposing flankers. Alternatively, he can hold the ball, draw an opponent or two, and then supply the scrum-half with possession of a higher quality than would otherwise have been the case. Again, if the circumstances warrant it, he has the power to initiate a wheel, presenting the opposition back row with a different set of problems. No number 8, in short, should be afraid to act decisively on his own judgement of what move should be adopted next.

If possession were lost and the opposition broke near the scrum, my own role was always to tackle the second attacker in the movement, probably going higher than usual and attempting to turn or rob him as swiftly as possible. But all teams, and in particular back rows, must plan a defensive system that works for themselves – and it needs to be really water-tight. For when it breaks down, as ours did when Wales played Scotland in 1973 and England in 1974, the consequences may be disastrous and your opponents can scamper in for short-range tries.

Those experiences helped to cement in my mind the idea that the number 8 cannot divorce his own activities from those of the two men flanking him: the three need to think and act as a unit. A good example of concerted work was the play of South Africa's back row in 1970, comprising a chopper-down in Greyling, Ellis the deft touch-player, and Bedford between them, knitting together their divergent skills. I was happiest playing alongside a big flanker like Quinnell or Peter Dixon, with speed-merchants such as Taylor or Slattery on the other, open side flank.

Moving on to the line-out, I do not have to emphasise how a tall number 8 can be the provider of precious quality possession for his team, either by a careful steering down (not flapping) of the ball to his scrum-half or by a clean catch. The latter is a valuable and sadly neglected skill these days, which both delays the opposing flankers' movement towards one's own halves and also, by prolonging the line-out, causes the enemy three-quarters to hold back lest they infringe the 10-metre law.

However, one thing I would like to underline is the importance of good throwing-in from touch, which during my time has been one of the poorest features of our game. I often ask myself why coaches do not spend more time discovering which of their players does it best. The job is usually given to hookers or wingers, but if a prop or flanker demonstrates at practice that he can perform it accurately, why should he not become his team's regular thrower-in? The best line-out possession comes from the number 5 or number 7 jumper, but the longer the throw, the greater the degree of precision needed. So it is worth seeking out the best candidate for the job, even if this calls for some slight reorganisation elsewhere.

A great deal of gamesmanship and crafty jockeying for position goes on at the tail of the line-out, which is, incidentally, the only place where that direct 'confrontation' — a term beloved of critics and analysts — takes place between rival number 8s. Here I enjoyed many a stirring battle with opponents like Ripley, Telfer, Hefin Jenkins, Sutherland of New Zealand and the two great Frenchmen, Dauga and Walter Spanghero. But elsewhere in the action a clash between two number 8s takes place only by accident, depending on how the broken play develops.

Mind you, when it does happen the result can be dramatic and can yield great satisfaction to the man who comes out on top. To digress for a moment, the Wallabies who visited Britain in the winter of 1975-6 included a strapping, twenty-two-year-old number 8 called Mark Loane, and although injury kept him out of the tourists' fixtures with my club, Swansea, and with Wales, people kept telling me, 'Merv, this fellow's a real threat to your status as the best in the business.'

So when he reported fit for Australia's end-of-tour match at Cardiff against the Barbarians, whom I was to captain, I licked my lips with relish. 'There is positively no way', I told myself as I trotted onto the pitch, 'that this youngster is going to have a good game today.' Sure enough, midway through the second half, I put him down with a really heavy tackle on the thigh as he was in the act of breaking between the Baa-Baas' centres. After getting up he hobbled around a bit awkwardly for five minutes before chucking it in and making way for a replacement.

That night, on the eve of the Wallabies' departure for home, I slapped him on the back with a consoling gesture. 'One day, Mark', I told him, 'you could be the top number 8 in the world. Not, however, while I'm around.' I had my tongue in my cheek, for in truth I regarded him as an outstanding prospect, who could quickly have become world-class as a member of a Wales or New Zealand eight.

That story brings me to consideration of the number 8's role away from the set-pieces, where the most important preliminary precaution is a very fast look at what is going on before deciding which course to follow into the open field. A tenth of a second scanning the scene is never time wasted, for it helps one in the vital business of anticipating how the play will develop. In attack the move called by one's backs should have been heard and understood, making support that bit easier, but of course they are at liberty to change their plans and a back-row forward can make himself that little bit more useful if he is quick to realise that something different is afoot.

Anticipation is even more important in defence, when intelligence, experience and native cunning must all be brought to bear on what the attacking side has in mind. A number 8 must teach himself how to recognise a scissors attack in its early stages, how to pick out a full-back moving forward to join his three-quarters, when to watch for a wing beginning his run-in from the narrow side. In that fraction of a second's scrutiny which I advocate, the brain must function like a mini-computer to work out just where a breakdown is likely to occur and where support will be needed.

Of course, the best computers can be defeated by the human factor, such as the genius possessed by a side-stepper like Gerald Davies, or an unpredictable opponent like Gareth Edwards, who persists in popping up in all the wrong places as far as a defence is concerned. But there are days when very accurate guide-lines can be established: the last time I played against Llanelli my knowledge of their liking for scissors and crash-ball manoeuvres enabled me to reap a rich harvest of midfield tackles, and after knocking Ray Gravell over for the tenth time I was grimly satisfied to hear him groan, 'Not you again, Davies! Don't you ever give up?'

Frequently I used to find myself the second forward to reach a breakdown, just behind men like John Taylor, Slattery, or Neath's perpetual-motion man Dai Morris. When this is the case, a number 8 may find himself put immediately in possession as the result of an opponent having been quickly robbed. If so, the choice is between driving further himself or serving a waiting half-back. Otherwise he helps form a maul to which he adds weight and skill in the attempt to secure the ball and allow a fresh wave of attacks to speed on their way.

It is for contributions I was able to make to mauling and rucking that I am quite happy to be remembered as far as attacking is concerned — not for great runs in the open or for regular try-scoring. Both my two tries for Wales came, in fact, from short range: the first, as I noted earlier, was a tail-of-the-line-out effort; the second, also from the line, came after supporting a thrust by Dai Morris and amazing everyone (including myself!) with a sprint that snatched the touch-down under the nose of that pacy Englishman Dave Duckham. My try for the Barbarians, which robbed the All Blacks of a hundred-per-cent record on their brief 1974 tour, also looked like a short-range job, but it actually owed much to a long, stamina-sapping run of some 60 metres in support of a break by the backs. However, a score such as that was a gratifying reward for all the conscientious support work one tried to put in backing up less fruitful moves.

Snapping up a try, though, was a bonus, for I never set out to be a glamorous, eye-catching number 8 and preferred to be relatively unobtrusive as far as spectators were concerned. That is why some admirers may have found me a little ungracious in accepting sincere compliments. For if a supporter commented in the club house, 'Great game today, Merv!' I would feel troubled, asking myself why I had attracted attention. Was it because I hadn't been getting stuck in?

So the only compliments which pleased me deep down were about my tackling. At a rough count forty of the tackles I made for Wales were vitally important ones, but only the most perceptive critics consistently acknowledged the effect they had had on the outcome of a game. It is a fact of life that try-scoring, not try-prevention, is what brings spectators to their feet and sets tongues wagging. So a budding number 8 who takes my game as a model for his own must learn to be philosophical about the amount of limelight in store for him; but he will obtain untold personal satisfaction, I promise him, if he perfects his tackling, from all angles and in all circumstances.

It is for the reader to decide how successful I have been at describing and delineating the number 8 game as I played it. The message I have tried to put across, in sum, is all about initiative and enterprise, which number 8 forwards need to show more than almost anyone else on the field. Often they will have opportunities, which they should not hesitate to grasp, of exerting near-total control of the game's course (which is an important reason why they frequently make good captains). With a bit of imagination they can set up moves which will catch the opposition napping; with foresight they can plug a gap through which attackers threaten to pour.

Notice finally, please, that I have made out a case for number 8s to be recognised as members of rugby football's intelligentsia! To anyone who scoffs at the idea, be he Barry John or your third XV stand-off half, reply with feeling, 'Number 8s are not donkeys!'

9 Behind the Shop Window: The Clubs

David Parry-Jones

Outsiders from as far afield as Auckland, Cape Town, Edinburgh or Twickenham often comment that the unique element in Welsh rugby is its spirit, whether manifested in the displays of its representative XV on the field or in the feverish support from the side-lines at Cardiff Arms Park.

That spirit almost certainly springs from the geographic unity of the Welsh scene. Although the gospel has now penetrated to most parts of the principality, the *hwyl* reaches its most frenetic in the south and east, where at most the distance separating the eighteen or twenty pre-eminent clubs is the seventy miles between Newport and Llanelli.

This means that players and supporters are in constant touch during the week. A Pontypool forward may be employed at the same factory as a Newbridge back; Maesteg committee-men can use the same local as their opposite numbers from Bridgend; Swansea fans work in the same steelworks as rivals from Neath, Aberavon or Llanelli. Inter-club games are thus no more than the Saturday consummation of seven days' intimate discussion and argument, boast and counter-boast, threat and apologia.

There is also an historic unity, born of parallel growth. Neath, Llanelli, Swansea, Newport, Cardiff and Aberavon were all founded in the half-decade following 1871. Later, at the turn of the century, Cross Keys, Ebbw Vale, Pontypool and Abertillery were formed within an eighteen-month period. Relationships between such sides thus have their origins near the dawn of Welsh rugby; and as time goes by they are continually cemented by frequent contact between senior officials, who may first have played against each

other as teenagers and whose friendship has flowered at local derbies spread over a quarter of a century and more.

The task of accounting for the development of the club
framework in Wales and the hold exerted by rugby football over
the urban Welshman awaits the sociologists, or possibly the
Aberystwyth historians who sat down in 1974 to begin work on
the official history of the game's first hundred years in the principality. So far Wilfred Wooller has probably come as close to the
answer as anyone in writing that rugby football ' . . . expressed the
turbulent effervescence of the race and provided an ideal substitute
for the warring instincts of years gone by'. And in truth, to men
lured down from the hills and crammed by an industrial revolution
into coal-mines and ironworks, the appeal of an open-air arena with
ample space for an afternoon's vigorous, combative sport must have
been irresistible. In due course the formation of rugby clubs tapped
the traditional tribal loyalties of the Welshman and gave him an
identifiable focal point of dedication.

And over the years his club has become his castle. With room to
breathe and relax, with pictures on the wall of distinguished
ancestral figures, with panels bearing the names of illustrious
predecessors, the rugby club-house has bestowed upon miners and
steelworkers a sense of continuity, dignity and exclusivity difficult
to feel in the often ruined industrial environment outside. It is here
that they have been able to give expression to their personalities and
stand on equal terms with doctors, lawyers and schoolmasters. From
here springs Welsh rugby's reputation as a game for all classes – and
that unified spirit which so impresses itself upon visitors to the country.

Some of Mervyn Davies's formative years were spent with London Welsh, a club which is out on a limb and whose character has
often struck people in the homeland as a little alien. Is it not, indeed,
affiliated to the ruling body of English rugby? Yet anyone who has
stepped inside the shining new portals of the London Welsh RFC
and paused to sniff the atmosphere or listen to the accents can be in
no doubt that here is a patch of foreign soil that is forever Wales. It
caters not only for exiles who have put down roots in the London
area, but also for birds of passage like Merv the Swerve, who gain

valuable career experience in the metropolis before returning to Wales. Happy the man who has known both the cavalier approach of Old Deer Park and the all-consuming intensity of a premier South Wales club like Swansea. He has tasted Welsh club rugby to the full.

MERVYN DAVIES

Although I was privileged to experience all the honours and excitement that rugby football has to offer, I still feel cheated when I reflect on the abrupt way in which my career ended. Why? Because I never had the chance to end my rugby days with a season or two in our second-class game in Wales.

I can imagine you saying to yourself, 'Nonsense! He played on the world's great pitches in front of crowds numbering scores of thousands. His team-mates and opponents included some of the finest players the game has known. He knew adulation and respect. How could he possibly have derived any pleasure from the knock-about hurly-burly of, say, the West Wales league? For once Merv doesn't know what he's talking about!'

Just wait a moment and let me explain. All right, I agree that first-class rugby, especially at International level, is the eight-cylinder version of the game. Certainly playing for the Lions and Wales was the most important thing in my rugby life, and I suspect I would have been heart-broken had my country ever dropped me. In the company of top players it is possible for collective expertise and accomplishment to reach immense heights, and you will have gathered by now that it affords me supreme satisfaction to look back at the peaks of achievement I and my contemporaries scaled.

I concede, too, that had I been able to continue for another season or two with Swansea and Wales I might well have hung my boots up forthwith and made a quick, complete break from the playing side of the game. However, I like to think that I might have chosen to follow the example set by my former back-row colleague, Dai Morris, the winner of thirty-four caps but yet a man who, on finishing with Neath, accepted the captaincy of his home village Rhigos and devoted himself to inspiring and encouraging the young hopefuls of the upper Neath Valley.

They have a grand social life up there at the Plough Inn, return-ing for sing-songs and bar-room chat after tough fixtures with local rivals like Glynneath and Blaengwrach. Dai is careful not to dominate the gatherings, in which he is treated not as a star flank forward but as one of the boys; but I know that Rhigos welcome the advice and the know-how he can contribute, and they value his sheer presence even more.

A top International player, you see, sometimes experiences a crisis of identity. He is fêted wherever he goes. He gets endless free pints and slaps on the back. There are always folk who hang upon his every word. But occasionally he is bound to ask himself, 'Is it Mer-vyn Davies the man who has earned all this popularity, or simply Mervyn Davies the rugby super-star?'

At Rhigos Dai Morris no longer experiences the kind of doubts I mention, for he swiftly discovered that he is in demand for his per-sonal qualities. In the second-class clubs (perhaps 'district' is a description they would prefer) a man finds his level, and if he wins acceptance he can be sure it is for the very best reasons. Here the social side of the game is, if not quite paramount, at least as import-ant as what happens on the field of play. Here you find the nuts and bolts, the nitty-gritty, call it what you like, of the whole rugby game.

I admit that I am not sure whether I would have had the strength of character to end my playing days as Dai has done; but in case you doubt my credentials for starting my reflections on club rugby at this rather modest level, let me emphasise that I spent three very hard years' apprenticeship with Swansea Training College com-peting against the tough customers who played for local clubs. We may have been 'college boys' and ostensibly better educated than opponents from places like Tumble, Amman United, Swansea Police (hard men, like all coppers!) or Lampeter, but we had to draw upon every last ounce of cunning and common sense to survive in such egalitarian company!

So many lessons had to be absorbed in those days, notably how to look after yourself in a forward struggle. You learned how to deal with a boot planted on the instep as you prepared to jump at a line-out. There would be jerks of the arm as you prepared to receive a pass, a sly tug at the jersey or an ankle tap as you sized up a tackle. Sometimes, if you were doing too well, you might suffer a no-nonsense punch on the nose while the referee's gaze was elsewhere — and it usually was, for in these games most of the rugby was played where the ref. wasn't!

You learned to soak up legitimate bruisings and batterings without complaining, and to hand something out in return. You learned to respect opponents who seemed to be a uniform 6 feet tall and 14 stone and each possessed sharp elbows and bony knees. Many of them sported crew-cuts, which emphasised the hardness of their heads, and liked to play with sleeves rolled up to reveal muscular forearms. They were men of steel, who made uncompromising opponents.

My only trip to hospital as a direct result of a rugby injury came while I was at college. Some mean little man broke my jaw in a game at King George V playing fields. Singleton Hospital was a mere 100 yards away, and I expected that I should be treated rapidly and without bother. The snag was that we had been playing on the morning of an International, which all the doctors had gone off to Cardiff to watch! There was nothing for it but a 10-mile drive to the Morriston Hospital accident ward on the other side of the city, something I do not recommend if your jaw is hurting like fury! Once there I still had to wait five hours for the result of X-rays, so I did not even have the consolation of viewing the International on television.

However, our opponents were by no means all brawn and no brain. Quite often they would work an outstanding coarse rugby ploy on their college adversaries. I remember a game against Upper Cwmtwrch, for which we had to change at the village hall down in the valley before puffing our way up a steep slope to the hill-top rugby pitch. The Training College XV was perspiring its way along this tortuous route when we were surprised by the sound of a diesel engine. The tractor which overtook us was pulling a trailer on which sat the Upper Cwmtwrch team, happily nursing their energies *en route* to the kick-off! I cannot recall the result, but I am sure we were slower starters than our opponents that day.

Sometimes, though, students were capable of counter-moves

which also owed much to native cunning. At college we had a clever stand-off half called Peter Fay, who hailed from Brynamman. On the day of our annual fixture against them, Brynamman asked for Peter's release to play against us, a request to which we grudgingly agreed. There came a moment when our turn-coat colleague made a superb break through our ranks, and after ten side-steps, a swerve or two and a dummy was left with just the full-back to beat. I had, however, managed to cover across, and from a yard or so behind him called out as a last-gasp measure. 'My ball. Pete!' whereupon he, obeying the instincts of innumerable college training sessions, flipped me a perfect inside pass. Away went the ball to touch, to a chorus of inventive verbal abuse from the whole Brynamman XV!

Great days they were! – and now I regret not having time to pay more visits to the smaller clubs and savour their wonderful atmosphere. However, I do try to drop in occasionally at Bonymaen, for whom my younger brother Dyfrig is a flank forward. I imagine that it is possible for a man to sulk and nurse a grudge against a brother who collects all the honour and the glory, but far from showing the slightest bit of envy Dyfrig was always, it seemed to me, my number one fan. Nothing was too much trouble for him: for example, on my arrival back at Heathrow from an overseas tour he would always drive the family car up the M4 to make sure I received a proper welcome home. Perhaps indeed it is I who sometimes envy Dyfrig – for the companionship and sheer fun that he has always got out of his rugby with Bonymaen. Like me he was lucky in his choice of wife, and I know that Linda would always rather watch Dyfrig Davies play rugby than his big brother Merv–and rightly so!

West Wales, of course, is notable for its league system, and it is hard for me to avoid commenting on the debate that has been running in Wales for five or six years now, about the possible introduction of a league to the big circuit. I can see that it is most agreeable for sides like Seven Sisters and Kidwelly, who do not normally step into the limelight or number International players in their ranks, to show off cups or shields in their trophy collection to underline their success during the season just past. But I am more cautious when people argue that such incentives would add a desirable competitive edge to the friendly matches now played between the top clubs.

For let's get one thing straight – such games are not 'friendlies' at all! When Swansea take on Llanelli or Neath or Cardiff I can tell you that they are totally dedicated to emerging victorious, and it is inconceivable that playing for two league points could add anything to the participants' will to win.

On the contrary a league system might introduce a ruthlessness into the game that went beyond our present sporting ideal. Rugby Union football is a game that is played, watched and administered primarily for pleasure; victory is important, but in an amateur game it must always be no more than a close second to the enjoyment provided. Because of the undoubted success of the West Wales set-up I am not against leagues on principle (and the Scots seem fairly satisfied with their system). But I have yet to be convinced that our first-class circuit in Wales needs radical change, and am relieved that the clubs have shown themselves to be conservative on the issue.

The Welsh Rugby Union Challenge Cup competition is a different matter. Although Swansea's arch rivals Llanelli won it four times out of the first five seasons in which it was played for, I still consider it to be one of the great innovations of the seventies! It is a tournament in which the smaller clubs can have a tilt at the giants, and since what they lack in skill and finesse they compensate for with guts, endeavour and determination, the outcomes of such matches are often in doubt. Clubs like Whitland, Blaina, Rhymney and Pembroke have frequently dealt out shock-treatment to glamorous opponents like Neath, Cardiff, Llanelli and Ebbw Vale, while Swansea too have often been made to battle for survival.

I vividly remember an afternoon in the autumn of 1973 when the All Whites played a third round tie at Taffs Well, that pretty village nestling under the shadow of Castell Coch between Cardiff and Pontypridd. Two thousand folk turned out to shout for their heroes, who forced us to pull out all the stops for our 13-6 victory. Elwyn, youngest of the famous Williams footballing brothers, had gone up the valley for a final season or two of less demanding rugby than he had known at Cardiff Arms Park, and on this day he inspired a pack who simply swarmed around their bigger Swansea opponents, snapping at our heels and harassing us into elementary errors. It was an encounter which epitomised all the best that the Cup competition has to offer.

That day is also memorable because of a tradition they have at Taffs Well whereby the visiting captain has to drink the 'yard of ale', a long, awkwardly-shaped glass vessel containing over three pints. Having played student rugby in the Cardiff area with the local training college, our skipper Bob Dyer knew all about this particular hazard, and after a quick shower made himself exceedingly scarce. Hence his vice-captain, who happened to be myself, had to stand in. No records were broken, but I consider myself a stayer, so that after what seemed an eternity the 'yard' had been drained. I was left with a bloated stomach, a brand-new Barbarians' tie soaking and discoloured from drips of best bitter, and the rueful suspicion that for me at least the best of the day was over!

However, by observing that tradition the Swansea club acknowledged the excellence of Taffs Well's organisation and the warmth of their welcome. Our boys stayed on at the club-house enjoying the company of our vanquished hosts until late in the evening, which I feel was the best kind of compliment we could have paid them. Long may the Cup flourish and stimulate contact between the major clubs and those others who provide a matchless rugby education for youngsters and endless pleasure for players whose ambitions stop short of greater things.

The first of the two premier teams for whom I played was, of course, London Welsh, whose methodical approach to organising the playing of rugby football I have described earlier. As far as the social side is concerned, since Old Deer Park is now the main rallying point for all the Welsh in London I was able to meet an astonishing cross-section of folk. On an average Saturday night I might find myself in conversation not only with the enterprising milkmen and drapers who traditionally left Wales to make good in London but also with cabinet ministers, MPs, industrial tycoons, union leaders, barristers, stockbrokers, university lecturers, and, inevitably, teachers from far and wide.

The Welsh in exile love any excuse to get together, and the hard core would have descended on the club in any case to polish up their native tongue and catch up with gossip from the homeland. But certainly the calibre of our play in the early seventies pulled in stars from other walks of life, who would probably not have come along to watch football of a lesser quality. At one time we could field twelve International players, including eight British Lions: J. P. R. Williams, Gerald Davies, Jim Shanklin, John Dawes, Keith Hughes, Bill Hullin, Tony Gray, John Taylor, Mike Roberts, Geoff Evans, Jeff Young and myself — I hope I haven't left anyone out. In addition there was that clever Wales B stand-off half Bob Phillips, who surely must have won a cap or two had not poor eyesight made him prone to handling errors.

Having provided eighty minutes of cracking entertainment, it then became our turn to ogle famous visitors. Sir Geraint Evans liked to come and see us play. That fine actor from Garnant, Hywel Bennett, lived near Old Deer Park and often dropped in for a pint. On one evening I noticed that I was rubbing shoulders with a hugely expensive-looking mink coat, whose wearer turned out to be Elizabeth Taylor, in company with her husband of the day, Pontrhydyfen-born Richard Burton. I thought that the lady's drink would be some costly cocktail until I heard Richard call out to the barman, 'A pint for me and a half of whatever Liz is drinking.'

When I joined the club our headquarters were being rebuilt and extended. Until 1970 therefore, we changed for matches at Richmond Baths, from where we rode in style by double-decker bus. (Our opponents always travelled on the upper deck — there was always a chance that, descending the stairs, one of them would do himself a mischief before the kick-off!) But in that year the Prince of Wales came to see a game against a selected Welsh XV, after which he performed the opening ceremony for our refurbished premises.

Saturday nights were always full of fun and variety. We could look forward to a hop, there was the possibility of excellent conversation with old London Welsh stalwarts like Ronnie Boon, Harry Bowcott or Dick Ellis, a fine club controller, or we might be entertained by soloists like Winston Bishop or visiting ensembles like the London Welsh Male Voice Choir. If we wanted to discuss the game we had just played, our first team organiser Len Davies, formerly of Swansea and Wales, would deliver some blunt home truths.

Even training nights were never a drag – once we had put behind us the spectre of Roger Michaelson whose job was to sharpen our fitness before handing over to John Dawes for coaching sessions. No player, however distressed he might become, escaped the lash of Roger's tongue. 'Don't sneak off into the trees to be sick,' he would bawl. 'Come and do it where we can all see.' This former Cambridge Blue, who won but one cap for Wales at number 8, was a really strong personality, whose cracking of the whip got the very best out of us. He was the kind of fanatic every club needs, a man you loved to hate, and he has since become a pillar of London Welsh's administrative structure.

What made things so much more enjoyable was the fact that we were winning matches. Admittedly the big crowds we drew everywhere usually came in the hope of seeing our colours lowered, as at the Middlesex Sevens where our successful sides were often booed by the very English Twickenham supporters. But most of the time people fell over themselves to bid us welcome.

Sometimes their anxiety to play us led them to transgress the bounds of common sense. A Gwent club once let us travel all the way from London on a Saturday morning only to find that the pitch was frost-bound and hard as iron. Although we realised that they had hoped against hope for a thaw towards mid-day, so that the bumper crowd they expected would materialise, we still felt hard-done-by, particularly those of us who had had to rise from bed at 7 am! Our general disenchantment at a wasted day touched untold heights when Tony Gray, dispatched to buy beer for the return journey at Newport's station buffet, took too long and missed the train.

Good rugby, though, and great companionship: these were the qualities for which I shall remember my days at Old Deer Park and because of which I always try to call there when I'm in town. It may strike some as a rather narrowly based existence, but as far as I was concerned it supplied every ingredient of social and sporting life that a man in his early twenties could desire.

Thus I strayed but seldom, usually for a game with Surrey in the English County Championship. Welshmen in London rarely turned down a chance to represent their adopted county, for it made a change. But on the whole I consider that the practice yielded doubtful benefits. Personally, I could never get excited about the result, and with a few shining exceptions like Martin Turner, the county organisers were not too clued-up. Such matches might profitably be reserved for properly qualified Englishmen rather than stars from foreign countries.

Even playing for London Counties left me rather cold. We were a disorganised side when the Springboks beat us 22-6 in 1970, and although another game against a Paris XV was won well, it turned out to be one of the few major débâcles of my personal career. They had made me captain, but since my grasp of French was rudimentary the fluent Ken Kennedy managed to exert the dominant role through rapid-fire exchanges with the referee which I could in no way follow. Ken, however, utterly failed to persuade this third-rate official to bring some order to a rough-house which I claim we lost 3-2 – Paris had two badly injured men off the field at the final whistle, London had three!

London Welshmen did have an appetite for county rugby though, in that our club played only on Saturdays and confined its fixtures to some thirty-five per season. An extra half dozen games in mid-week for Surrey, plus a Trial or two and four representative matches for Wales added up to a total that struck me as exactly right. I respect a man who is willing to take the field more often, but to play fifty, sixty or more times a season is surely misguided.

When I moved back to Swansea, though, pressure to play a lot more rugby was the principal difference I experienced from the London scene. By the 1972-3 season I was a pretty confident performer, who knew what was good for him and when a rest was needed. I suspect that I quickly won something of a reputation with our supporters as a chooser of my games. So be it; but people really ought to appreciate that an International player needs to husband and nurse his resources in preparation for representative matches that will make extremely heavy demands upon him. Certainly those All Whites who won caps in the mid-seventies, Geoff Wheel, Mark Keyworth, Trevor Evans and Roger Blyth, are now in a position to support my case.

I must add my general view, too, that unfair demands are made upon leading Welsh players during the season. Club committees are partly to blame, and have used the spread of floodlights as an excuse for mounting extra mid-week games which keep their finances healthy. But players, too, could take steps to cut down on the amount they play. I know that Gareth Edwards has had to take some stick at Cardiff for having the courage to tell his selection committee 'not available' from time to time, but if more men followed his example our national team would be that much fresher and keener at the start of the Five Nations Championship campaign. How many Welshmen realise that All Blacks like Going or Kirkpatrick may play as few as thirty-two games a year: twenty for their club, half a dozen for the provincial XV, a couple of Trials and maybe four Tests? Could not such restraint be a major reason for their achievements down the years?

Again, it is fashionable to scoff at the Dad's Army which turns out year in year out for Ireland. But there is nothing wrong with maturity in rugby if we are to judge by the consistent form shown by 'oldies' like Kiernan, McBride, McLoughlin and Gibson. The point is, I suggest, that their longevity can be traced to playing less often. It amuses us in Wales; but we should bear in mind that some of our stars are burned out by the time they are twenty-seven or twenty-eight. The clubs ought not to allow this to happen: however important the game may be, its players should always receive prime consideration.

Admittedly, men in their early twenties are frequently keen enough to want two or three outings a week, and will appear to take them in their stride. I commend them for their enthusiasm, while simply warning them that staleness is an inevitable result, and that they will be physically unable to contribute the one-hundred-per-cent effort that every match demands.

Having got these points off my chest I must now make it clear that the Swansea club could not have been more understanding about my position and my views. Furthermore, they certainly came up trumps during my period in hospital and subsequent convalescence during 1976. They went to great lengths to allay all concern I felt about routine affairs like the well-being of my family, so that Shirley and my parents never had to worry about a lift to Cardiff to pay me a visit. My ward was always full of baskets of fruit lavished upon me by the ladies' committee, while at Gorseinon Hospital the supporters' club made a colour television set available to me. And I feel sure that Swansea would have accorded similar treatment to any player who had suffered some mishap, whether he happened to be a British Lion or a Second XV reserve. I applaud, too, the way in which Pontypool and Neath have attended to the needs of their hospitalised players Roger Addison and Keith Morris. Unfortunately Roger can rarely leave his ward at Rookwood, but I have spotted Keith more than once in his wheel-chair on the Gnoll touch-line, savouring some attacking thrust by the All Black forwards. Sometimes I get invitations to join Rotary or the Masons. I usually reply that I am already a member of the greatest freemasonry in the world: Welsh club rugby.

In my time Swansea never quite pulled off a major title, though we did reach the Cup Final in 1976. It was one of my two great disappointments at St Helen's that I was not fit to lead them that day; the other was the previous autumn when we went down 12-6 to the Wallabies, whom we could have beaten had we been less inept. That was the match in which Paddy Batch was sent off after a heavy tackle on Bob Dyer. I considered the decision harsh.

But there was a great deal of good rugby too, probably of a better standard than had been seen at St Helen's for some seasons. During the early seventies coaching there was in the hands of Ieuan Evans, who had come to Swansea after doing great things for Llanelli; and round about the time I arrived from London, the young team that he had been nurturing reached fruition and we became a power in the land. In addition to the lead set by our crop of Internationals – Wheel, Phil Llewellyn, Keyworth, Blyth and Trevor Evans – there were splendid contributions from Neil Webb, Roger Hyndman, Bob Dyer, veteran Mike James and wings Gwynfor Higgins and Gerwyn Jones, while a long-standing problem at stand-off half was solved by the arrival of the brilliant young secondary schools cap, David Richards. These were men of talent and endeavour, whom it was a pleasure to lead in my final season.

Ieuan Evans left the club in 1974, and inevitably onlookers

wondered why. It is no secret, I suppose, that he and I did not see eye-to-eye on certain issues. However, just as Clive Rowlands knew after six years that he had given all he had to offer to the national XV, I believe that Ieuan too came to realise that he needed a fresh challenge, and that it would not pay him to remain in what could have become a stagnant situation at Swansea. A strong personality, he quickly became a vice-president of the WRU, and continued to hold the important post of coach to the Wales Youth XV, so he still had opportunities for expressing his particular rugby flair. Nor was I surprised one afternoon at Neath, after watching a fine display by the home side against Pontypool, to learn that he had been along to the Gnoll to take a couple of coaching sessions.

Ieuan was succeeded at Swansea by Stan Addicott, a member of the younger generation, who never experienced the problems of communication which had often beset his predecessor. I would suggest that as a general rule clubs should appoint recently retired players as coaches; Clive Rowlands once confided in me near the end of his reign as Wales coach, 'It's so long since I played the game I've forgotten what it's all about.' He may have been ex-aggerating a little: what he really meant was that rugby was going through a period of very rapid change. But in contrast John Dawes, who took control in 1974, had been active with London Welsh as late as 1972 and had no such hang-ups about being out of touch.

The men I grew to like and respect at St Helen's included Judge Rowe Harding, a sort of senior citizen and general overseer at the club, Eddie Rickard, our trusty baggage man, and that faithful bus driver Tony Clements who could never quite find his way to Pontypool! Because of his care and concern at the time of my collapse I acknowledge a debt to our honorary club doctor, Gordon Rowley, and also to Viv Davies, in whom Swansea possessed a forceful chairman and dynamic front-man.

But then, such key figures are to be found wherever in the world organised rugby is played. And, looking back, all the clubs I visited, great and small, had distinctive characteristics and personalities of their own making them attractive to visit and play against. During my stay at Old Deer Park I always looked forward to local derbies against London Irish and London Scottish, which were often of a ferocity that put me in mind of West Wales vigour! At Richmond or the Harlequins one normally had to aim for a higher standard of behaviour than usual, but the beer was good. Coventry was a pleasure to visit, not least because one could renew acquaintance with fellow tourists like Dave Duckham and Geoff Evans, and if I have one regret as far as the English club scene is concerned it is that I scarcely ever made it down to Devon and Cornwall where the hospitality is out of this world.

In Wales I particularly enjoyed being at Stradey Park, where the rugby was hard, but where afterwards players were whisked away from public pressures to a small bar where we could spend a quiet half-hour chatting among ourselves before the confrontation with the fans. Cardiff Arms Park, too, always had a special aura about it. But these are only two clubs out of a dozen or fifteen with whom it was always a pleasure to renew rivalry.

One club, finally, which fits into no particular category is the Barbarians FC, that unique band who don't have a home and, like a troupe of performing minstrels, tour the land bent on providing spectacular entertainment and spreading the gospel of rugby for fun. There are certain aspects of the Baa-Baas' approach of which I approve whole-heartedly, such as the opportunity afforded to young, inexperienced men to play next to Lions and seasoned International stars. An uncapped player is traditionally included in the XVs for end-of-tour games with premier overseas sides like Australia, against whom Mike Knill appeared in 1976, and New Zealand, whose opponents included Bob Wilkinson for the 1973 clash.

That game was immortalised, of course, by The Try which Gareth Edwards scored after six team-mates had handled in a move which swept 75 yards upfield, and in any other contest at such a level it would never have been 'on'. Had he been playing for Wales, Phil Bennett, who started it all with three dazzling side-steps, would certainly have put in a safe line-kick from what was potentially a suicidal position on his own 25. But that day, imbued with the Barbarian spirit, he reached out for glory.

It is true, also, that I scored the most satisfying try of my career in the Barbarians' colours, against New Zealand at Twickenham in autumn 1974. Since it turned out to be my last game against the

'Blacks' it is satisfying to have left them with that final defiant gesture. Yet, except against the very highest quality opposition, the Barbarians' style of play did not have overwhelming appeal for me, and I occasionally declined invitations to represent the club since I felt that other men were available whose talents were more suitable for happy-go-lucky, abandoned rugby football. I was especially glad to have opted out of the meeting with Fiji at Gosforth in 1970 when the tourists won 29-9!

My other observation on the Baa-Baas concerns their exclusivity. Great players from Wales like Norman Gale, Clive Rowlands and John Taylor were consistently overlooked during their illustrious careers. They can be forgiven for considering it something of an honour not to have received a call-up into the Barbarians' ranks.

I will conclude by citing Ray Williams's view that rugby football's shop window, which attracts the gaze of sight-seers and excites their imagination, is International play, and to be part of the glittering display mounted by Wales was the prime delight of my career. But the goods have to be produced somewhere; and it is in the clubs, at all levels, that are to be found the assembly plants and conveyor belts which throw up a Barry John, a Gareth Edwards, a Gerald Davies, or a Terrible Eight.

10 *Slings, Arrows and Aggro*

David Parry-Jones

At its higher levels, where degrees of skill and accomplishment vary but little, rugby football is a game of moods. All things being equal, the side whose players take the field with untroubled minds, totally attuned to the business in hand, is the side which will emerge on top. That is what coaches have in mind when they employ the term 'motivation', which means not only the injection of an all-consuming will to win but also a putting-aside of all distracting thoughts and considerations.

Coincidentally, however, the coaches' task is made harder, because for as long as a week before a big match they will deliberately have indulged in a tension-creating exercise designed to unleash their players upon the opposition like a tightly coiled spring. Thus any extraneous irritant, which in another context would be of less crucial importance, is capable of diminishing the potency of men whose temperament is at its most vulnerable and whose nerves are nothing if not highly strung.

Sometimes the irritant – or 'aggro', as Mervyn Davies chooses to call it – may be unattributable to any human failing, or simply unavoidable. After one of his rare poor performances for Wales, against New Zealand in 1973, Phil Bennett confessed that he 'didn't want to know' and ought not to have taken the field at all. He and his wife had just suffered the loss of a baby who died at birth. Perhaps that was an occasion when a senior adviser should have insisted that Phil withdrew from an encounter to which clearly he had no chance of feeling fully committed.

But other, far less significant factors can also undermine a man's mood and morale. A dressing-room is too cramped and claustrophobic. A jersey feels too tight about the chest and shoulders. A muscle will seem to give twinges, real or imaginary, which lead its owner to wonder uneasily if it will 'pull' during the game. Outside, the wind may be strong or gusting, diluting the confidence of a player whose dead-ball or line-kicking is important to his team. There may be frost patches here and there on the pitch: nothing so diminishes a man's appetite for further physical involvement than a really painful landing early in a game. Foul tactics by the opposition can provide an incentive to retaliate wildly, with players bent on vengeance rather than constructive rugby. A bad decision by the referee, or the feeling that he is officiating inconsistently, may deflate the zest of a whole team. And, back in the club-house after it is all over, an unnecessarily cutting remark by an official or committee-man sometimes leaves a player nursing a grievance for a whole week, or even prompts him to move to another club.

'Such things are all in the mind,' the cynic may observe. But rugby players, in the main, are no more than pleasant, straightforward youngsters out for an afternoon's fun, yet who may be required to exercise a high degree of self-control in a competitive, combative situation.

How much harder can it be for them to come to terms with the host of professional critics whose job it is to report rugby in the Press or on radio and television. Let us assure players of one thing: most of these men are in the business because of a basic delight in the game and a desire to promote it. For this reason they seek to show its participants in a genial, often flattering light; and, equally, they are fully aware of players' sensibilities. They defer to the man of twenty-nine, still with an outside chance of the coveted cap, who beseeches them to stop referring to him as a 'veteran' lest the selectors' minds should be swayed against him. They humour the twenty-seven-year-old with receding hair who asks them not to describe him as the 'balding lock'. They deal gently with the belligerent young hopeful, yet to be glamorously written-up, who asks menacingly, 'What have you got against me?'

Rugby writers and broadcasters, fallible though they may be, have one thing in common. Because of their love for the game they are constantly seeking to praise quality and expertise. When they criticise — and they know that what they write will sometimes wound — it is more in sorrow than in anger. They are perfectly prepared to defend an opinion, so long as acrimony is kept out of the argument, and if an improvement takes place as the result of something they have said or reported they are well pleased.

The decade during which I have covered rugby football in Wales has provided few occasions for severe criticism. Club rugby in general has reached a commendably high standard, while at International level writers have usually been left to analyse why a Welsh XV did not score another 20 points, not why they lost. This has led some players and officials to grumble that comment in the media has become tendentious and carping, but they miss the point: as the standards they set themselves have risen, so the level of criticism has adjusted itself to the new excellence on display. At Twickenham in 1976, when Wales made heavy weather of overcoming a rugged challenge by England 21-9, the media were actually kinder than the national team coach, who said bluntly, 'We played badly.'

Innumerable newspaper-cuttings make it clear that Mervyn Davies got a consistently good Press wherever he played in the world. The tightness of his chosen style largely eliminated mistakes, and if he was ever guilty of errors of judgment they were never so glaring that rugby writers could make capital out of them. People never wrote that Merv was over the top.

Even if they had, one doubts if it would have disturbed the equilibrium of a man whose temperament and iron will-power were admirably suited to a game which, to all appearances, is volatile and tempestuous, but in which the man who keeps his cool emerges with the spoils. I suppose that deep within him flickered the doubts and uncertainties that beset all who aim for greatness and become pre-eminent; and in the course of protracted conversations with me he once admitted, 'All of us like to be told now and then that we are good.'

But Mervyn Davies's private armour was strong, his heart was stout, and — until that last outrageous stroke — he was well equipped to resist the slings and arrows of fortune.

MERVYN DAVIES

Bob Hiller, an opponent for whom I had deep respect and affection, used to take more than his fair share of stick from hostile crowds, who regularly lost their patience at the deliberate and time-consuming preparations he made for kicks at goal. Through it all, however, he remained ultra-calm, sometimes even hitting back with crushing retorts of his own.

Once, in New Zealand, he was spending his usual minute and a half digging a hole and using the soil for a 3-inch tee 40 yards from the posts, when a spectator bawled, 'Put a move on, Hiller! What do you want – a shovel?' Bob paused to reply, 'No. Just lend me your mouth!' Then, to add injury to insult, he coolly placed the goal.

Barry John also possessed an ice-cold temperament. There was another New Zealand occasion when a partisan Hawkes Bay crowd at Napier had flung every verbal missive in the book at the Lions in an attempt to sap our confidence and force us into errors – all to no avail, for we won comfortably 25-6. Near the end the 'King' found himself with the ball in an open space, but with no opponent making a move to challenge him. So he calmly stood still. Then, as spectators raged and fumed, he deftly rolled the ball from one hand to the other behind his back before putting in a long, rolling touch-kick that gained us 40 yards. A supreme gesture of contempt for a crowd to which we had not warmed in the least.

As an International player I placed a high premium on the cultivation of such self-control. For although rugby football is a game full of tension and drama it is important to keep a cool head in the midst of all the aggro and petty provocation that take place. Some of it amounts to no more than a minor pin-prick for which nobody is to blame; there is another variety which is malicious and often pre-meditated. Either kind, however, is capable of disturbing a player's composure and single-mindedness, especially at representative level. I will tell you about some of the things that can happen and the influences that affect men's performances.

Let us return for a moment to crowd behaviour. The Argentina Test of October 1976 was the first in which I had not been a member of the Welsh XV since 1968, and in the grandstand I was much distressed at the booing which beset Gonzalo Becca-Varela as he prepared to kick a vital penalty goal. But my embarrassment was nothing compared with that which I knew our players on the field were experiencing. Whenever visiting place-kickers were booed at Cardiff in my time it made us ashamed to be Welsh for a few moments, which is the last feeling on earth you want when you are doing your best to beat the opposition to a frazzle. I am certain, too, that being hooted makes a kicker all the more determined to place the goal, so the crowd's bad manners may be doubly damaging to their heroes' chances.

Mind you, the roar of the Cardiff crowd is a tremendously unnerving sound to visiting players in the normal course of a game. From the field it has a curious vibrato quality, a continuous 'waa-waa-waa' booming into the ear-drums; and of course to invading teams it sounds like a non-stop war chant, reverberating hostility. Conversely, when Wales played away at grounds like Twickenham or Murrayfield, I tried to concentrate so hard as to be oblivious of the tumult of encouragement for the home side. Then it became no more of an ordeal than walking down a busy street, when you are aware of traffic noise without actually 'hearing' it.

Welsh singing, too, could undoubtedly depress the opposition and give a real lift to the men in red, though again, if I became acutely aware of it, I would take it as a danger sign that my concentration was flagging. Beware also, the Arms Park crowd that begins to sing too early in the game. This is often a pointer to underlying fears that Wales are up against it!

At International level I was never aware of individual pieces of encouragement or invective, but at club games some piercing and sarcastic voices would penetrate the general hubbub from time to time. A player having a bad game, who the Old Deer Park fans decided should not have been selected, might hear the spiteful catcall, 'Who's been buying gin and tonics for Harry Bowcott, then?'

The solemnity of representative fixtures means that players have to stand still for two or three minutes while anthems are played, and for some this inactivity was enormously trying. Our boys always sang *'Mae Hên Wlad fy Nhadau'* (including John Taylor, who had to be taught the words by a team-mate in time for his first cap, having been brought up in Watford!) and enjoyed hearing a stadium resound to Welsh voices. At the same time we all longed to take hold of the ball and get on with the game, a sure way of quelling any threatened attack of nerves. We feared that every second spent without moving diminished the benefit of important warming-up exercises done in the changing-room. To be quite candid, if you watch a Wales XV closely during the singing of the anthems you will see its members assume a posture that is almost droopy. Other teams might stand to attention like guardsmen, but we preferred to relax our limbs slightly, even surreptitiously flexing ankles and knees to keep them supple.

Some players, of course, need to sing and hear the anthem as a kind of final 'fix' to get them high on patriotism before clashing with the foe. Ray Gravell is such a man, and when at Dublin in 1976 the Welsh anthem was omitted as part of an exercise to play down off-the-pitch political tension, he and Geoff Wheel began to sing it on their own as a duet. The rest of us were able gradually to join in, being well within earshot; in my time Welsh sides formed what amounted to a huddle during the anthems, to prolong and intensify the togetherness we had striven to build up before taking the field.

One year there was a fuss at Twickenham, when the Rugby Football Union told the band to play only 'God Save the Queen', and the match began to a chorus of dissent and derision from thwarted Welsh songsters on the terraces. Afterwards people said that we players should have stood our ground until our anthem was played, but the truth is that we were too nonplussed at the time to contemplate such a thing. Although I would not ascribe our eventual defeat to this break with tradition, I recall that we certainly began the match on the wrong foot. A rare example, perhaps, of English cunning!

My final observation on the anthems ceremony: this is the time when players may be tempted to steal a glance at their opposite number, size him up, and maybe experience a tremor or two. After my daunting glances at Kirkpatrick and co. in 1969 I eschewed the practice; but if opposing number 8 forwards wished to look at me, that was their business. A line or two from Shakespeare sums up the impression I tried to convey: 'Stiffen the sinews, summon up the blood . . . then lend the eye a terrible aspect,' enjoins Henry V before Harfleur. Likewise Merv always tried to look fierce and flinty, and would probably be wearing two days' growth of beard to exaggerate a stern appearance. This was, to be honest, one reason why I grew my 'bandit' moustache. I shaved it off once in South Africa, only to decide that without it I was unable to 'disguise fair nature with hard favour'd rage'!

Once the action is under way there are many ways in which players may attempt quite legitimately to disturb the composure of their opponents. In one clash between Swansea and Neath my club scored three times in fairly quick succession, with the result that Neath kicked off three times running. On each occasion it fell to me to make the catch, under the nose of that hard prop Glyn Shaw, who was able to pick his target and drive into me in the vulnerable area between ribs and hip-bone. He hurt me, and must have guessed it, but I was determined not to give him the satisfaction of knowing for certain. So in each case I disguised the initial pain and waited until a subsequent lull in the play afforded a chance to rub the sore part of my anatomy. Hurting an adversary within the law is a perfectly fair way of making him less effective; but if he can come up smiling, or pretending to do so, then he has won the exchange.

There is a black list, mercifully very short, of men who in my opinion look forward to an afternoon's rugby chiefly for the chance it gives to maim an opponent. Some of them are the most inoffensive blokes off the field, and eyebrows would be raised if I named names. The game's essential brotherhood dissuades me from doing so; but that does not mean that I approve of the gouging, the pinching, the sinking of toe-caps into kidneys, and the boots or fists which come smashing through gaps deliberately created in the front row.

Raking at the ruck is something which outrages many players and spectators but which, curiously enough, I can accept. It is undeniably painful, though not quite as painful as it appears. However, the superficial scars it leaves soon heal, and at least it is basically carried out with the aim of obtaining possession by projecting the ball, plus any opponents near it, back in the direction of the scrum-half.

Kicking at rucks is far more culpable, since it may damage the victim's internal organs or break bones in his back or neck. In my opinion it usually merits a sending-off. It has the practical disadvantage, too, that if contact is made with the ball it will deliver possession into the hands of the other side. All Blacks, the world's best ruckers, never indulge in kicking.

Because of 'kickers', 'tramplers' and 'rakers', the ruck has, down the years, become a potent flash point for all kinds of aggro on the pitch, and partly for this reason there are many who argue that its days are now numbered. They say that players should be allowed to grapple for the ball when it is on the ground with hands and arms as they can now do at the maul (when it is in someone's grasp). Although New Zealand would probably resist such an innovation with might and main, since the ruck is so important a feature of their game, I might if pressed be prepared to support it. In the final analysis, rugby is supposed to be a handling game.

Much thinking would need to be done on how to rewrite the relevant laws. However, handling at the ruck would cut out much unnecessary pain and suffering, and the Jim Telfers of this world might be grateful for the change: Jim was a brave Scot with the courage to lie on any ruck ball that his country seemed in danger of losing, and after some games his back must have looked as if it had been lashed with the cat o' nine tails. As long as players like Telfer are allowed by referees to indulge in such unfair blocking, however, rucks will continue to provide the kind of frustration and exasperation which leads swiftly to violence and punch-ups.

Because it is so dangerous, the neck-high tackle must also be hounded out of rugby football. It is usually practised as a last resort by would-be tacklers who have been wrong-footed by a good side-step, and I know that sometimes it is done instinctively rather than with malice aforethought. When, however, the defender has time to stiffen his fore-arm and perhaps clench a fist, then it deserves severe punishment, since it could break an opponent's neck or put him out of the game for some weeks. Travaglini, Argentina's huge centre of the late sixties and early seventies, was a past-master of it,

G

and I am glad that his short-arm jolt of J. P. R. Williams in the closing seconds of the Cardiff Test in 1976 cost his country the match when Phil Bennett converted the resultant penalty. Short of being sent off, there can be no harder way of learning a common-sense lesson.

Great players, indeed good players at all levels, have no need to practise foul tactics, and if they are on the receiving end should resist the impulse to retaliate except as a very last resort. Colin Meads struck David Watkins and Jeff Young vicious blows in Tests for New Zealand; Brian Price laid out Noel Murphy; Ian Robinson broke All Black Jeff Matheson's cheek-bone at Cardiff. But if you analyse such incidents they were totally unnecessary in the context in which they took place, for they cannot be said to have influenced the respective results. I was no angel: but my advice to fiery players is to be more like a slow-burning fuse than an explosive device.

Consideration of dirty play brings me to the laws, and firstly to the old-established argument about differential penalties. It is certainly a source of anger and annoyance to many players that a technical offence like foot-up or a marginal off-side, attributable to over-eagerness or a misjudgment, is liable to the same punishment as a blatant punch or trip. Altering the law, though, to take account of the difference between the two kinds of infringement is not as easy as it sounds. For a start this would throw more responsibility upon referees, who already have a bewildering amount of detail to absorb and split-second verdicts to reach.

It is no good to suggest that they could receive assistance from touch judges. Law-makers have to bear in mind all levels of the game, and what might work at Cardiff Arms Park or Twickenham, where top-notch referees run the line, would be impracticable down the scale, where touch-judges are simply the most willing and amenable persons within call, and seldom qualified to advise the man with the whistle.

Another school of thought says that kicks at goal should no longer be allowed after technical offences, or should count for less. If the punishment were diminished, however, minor infringements might take place more frequently, with teams willing to concede a

penalty in order to regroup. Back-row forwards might make less of
an effort to stay on-side if they knew that their team stood to lose
nothing from stealing a march on the referee. No, a lot more
thought must be given to this issue before it is resolved.

I am relieved that, dating from the season following my retirement, referees began to be very strict on collapsers of scrummages. It
is extremely hard for an official to decide who exactly is to blame: a
front row may go to earth to protect its possession from an eight-
man shove, or to recover from a poor initial position. Alternatively,
it may be leaned on to such an extent by bigger adversaries that it
has no choice, for when half a ton-weight of effort is being applied
from behind retreat is not possible.

When, however, referees award penalties by rote as it were,
against each side in turn, front rows do make an effort to cut out the
collapsing, so hopefully the tragic crop of broken necks witnessed in
the mid-seventies will be the last to mar the game. More than that I
shall not say, for props and hookers are a different breed from the
rest of us, with a philosophy and a set of secrets all their own. A
team can leave the field downcast at a 30-0 defeat, yet their hooker
will be singing under the shower because he won the strikes against
the head by 2-1!

One law that has irritated me personally a great deal down the
years is that concerning the mark, or fair catch. I fail to see why a
team that puts up a well-judged 'Garryowen' should be denied advantage by an opponent who simply manages to catch the ball, and
then calls a temporary halt to the play. Since the catcher is at the
mercy of a determined following-up tackle, I would also write the
mark out of the law-book on grounds of safety.

Laws, on the whole, are not a source of aggro, and we have to
have them. I must say wistfully, though, that I wish there were
fewer of them! You would be surprised how often top International
players mutter incredulously to each other after some particularly
sharp blast on the whistle, 'What on earth was that for?'

One minor irritant which has disappeared from the game since
my father's time is that primitive monstrosity the leather stud, tack-
ed to the boot by small nails whose heads soon became sharp and
capable of inflicting nasty lacerations on soft flesh. I shudder to

think about it! But equally do I deplore modern plastic studs, whose edges tend to become as sharp as razors and which I consider should be banned in favour of the metal type.

The only other on-the-field source of aggro I can bring to mind falls into a slightly different category, and was a source of amusement to all save the victim. Early in a Test against Japan at Tokyo in 1975 I went slithering along the touch-line after a tackle, and within ten minutes my back felt as if it was on fire. After the game it transpired that the line had been marked out with lime, which had combined with the sweat of my body to form a painful alkali. The trouble was that our coach John Dawes decided that the alkali should be countered with a strong acid, and in the shower-room splashed half a bottle of after-shave lotion over the raw area. In no way was this a good idea! I am assured, by those who know, that 'Sid' is an excellent chemist; I can tell them one thing – he will never make a good doctor.

It is pleasant here to write off the Dawes style of medical assistance and pause to pay a sincere tribute to Wales's physiotherapist Gerry Lewis. Before a big game players have all kinds of muscular twinges, some real, some imaginary, and Gerry's rub-down in the changing-room was something we all savoured. He probably worked harder in the hour before the kick-off than any of his charges out on the park. My sole complaint is that he failed to keep 'Coco' Edwards at bay: one of our scrum-half's favourite wheezes was to give a painful twang to the elastic jock-strap of a team-mate who lay defenceless on the massage table!

There was no messing around on the pitch, though, where injured players trusted Gerry's judgment implicitly. Whatever pain we might feel, we knew that he would tell us whether it was safe to continue or whether we should make way for a replacement. He was, and is, a tower of strength.

Let us now stray further from the touch-line and consider the Press as a potential source of irritation. Rugby writers have a job to do, and I have learned to recognise that they are under pressure from editors to obtain 'stories' and spot 'angles' that have eluded their rivals. But in order to achieve these aims they are sometimes guilty of trapping young and inexperienced players into assertions or admissions which can lead to subsequent embarrassment or ill-feeling.

Speaking once to the assembled pupils at a New Zealand secondary school, I delivered a few home truths about lack of inventiveness in All Black rugby as I saw it. I probably exaggerated my points in order to emphasise the message and inspire the kids to go in for a creative style of play. But tucked away at the back of the hall there had been a reporter, and on the following day I was horrified to see towering headlines in the New Zealand newspapers: 'Merv Canes New Zealand Rugby', 'Merv Calls Our Rugby Boring'. Lions manager Doug Smith had me on the carpet for the indiscretion, and from that day forward I learned to guard my tongue in any gathering which was the least bit public. This stood me in good stead on occasions where alcohol was being served, for a few drinks can speedily loosen a young man's reserve and lead him to disclose things which some sharp-eared scribes delight to publish.

In their own company players do like to let off steam and pass opinions that they would hate to see in a newspaper, and Pressmen who try to foist themselves upon a private huddle are likely to get a very cold shoulder. Another habit which deserves the big brush-off is that of ringing players up late at night for a 'quote'. Because of this, although personally I was put under more pressure, I felt glad when in early 1976 the Welsh Rugby Union forbade reporters to contact any of the players under me during the period preceding an International match.

One or two writers broke a confidence with me during my career, but paid the penalty of never getting a subsequent interview. Others I have known deliver criticisms which are not only thoughtless and gratuitous but, more important, hurtful to sensitive players. However, if men of stature like New Zealand's Terry McLean or John Reason of the *Daily Telegraph* let fly with a barb or two then it is time to sit up and take notice. Over the years, too, I learned to trust Bryn Thomas of the *Western Mail,* even though I was not too pleased with the sentiments with which he greeted my entry into the Welsh side in 1969. Since retiring and sitting on the other side of the fence, I have enjoyed my association with Chris Lander, who helps me to shape and polish my weekly column for the *Daily Mirror*. I respected, too, the late Pat Marshall of the *Daily Express*, and felt greatly honoured to become the first recipient of the memorial award named after him. His defiant brand of English patriotism was something I could understand.

On the whole, player–Press relationships in Britain are good. And most of us, however enraged we may become about match reports we consider one-eyed or biased, treasure the things that are written about us, good and bad. I have several scrap-books bulging with cuttings which Shirley and my mother have somehow kept up to date. Browsing through them I am often agreeably surprised to find how kind journalists were to me as a player.

Television coverage of rugby I think of primarily for its entertainment value, which can be very high. In fact, at the top level I think rugby union football now provides the best winter sports entertainment available in Britain. Compared with our game, rugby league football has an irritating stop-start rhythm and is altogether too predictable. Association football has its supreme moments, interspersed with long periods when nothing seems to be happening. Television cameras, too, miss a lot of meaningful running off the ball, whereas in rugby the important action usually takes place where the ball is.

My main criticism of rugby as shown on television is that, in a thirty-minute edited version, a game's real character may be distorted. A team that scores five tries in the final twenty minutes of a match may have had to work really hard in the early stages to establish such superiority. Producers, however, bent on showing entertaining pictures, naturally show more of the rout and less of the hand-to-hand engagement, so that the calibre of the beaten side may look over-feeble. With that reservation, there is little doubt that the fans can feel satisfied with the coverage they get, especially in Wales where the televising of matches is in the hands of particularly expert men like Onllwyn Brace and Dewi Griffiths. The latter, incidentally, was a valued tour companion especially when he relinquished cutting and mixing shots to tickle a post-match keyboard.

Personally, I used to hate watching my own recorded performances on television, but it was always a worth-while exercise since I occasionally spotted some short-coming that I could put right. For the same reason the Welsh squad preparing for an International match liked to view its play in the preceding game. Contrary to popular opinion we rarely studied film of our prospective opponents in action, since we preferred to concentrate upon our own capabilities and decide how the match could best be controlled by us.

In Wales, rugby league scouts were once peddlers of a special kind of aggro. They badgered and harassed leading players with tempting cash offers, and damaged national morale by creaming off stars like Dai Watkins, Maurice Richards or John Bevan. In my time, however, their influence has waned, probably since our leading players no longer need to look north for personal or job security. We are made to feel appreciated by our public. I also believe that a heightened national consciousness has made men reluctant to turn their backs on Wales and depart to an alien environment. Many southern Welshmen have been disappointed on reaching the promised land, nor do I think that players like Chico Hopkins and Keith Jarrett ever really adapted to the new code.

Not once, by the way, did I receive an offer to go north, and for years I felt slighted when I heard of the huge cash incentives dangled in front of certain Welsh scrum-halves and full-backs! I have to admit, however, that the league scouts were right: my skills and expertise would have been far less relevant in a game which has no line-outs and no mauls. And on the whole I am glad that I spent my days in a code where the principal rewards lay in participation, not pay-packets. Long may rugby union remain an unpaid pastime.

Some folk, of course, allege that top Welsh players do receive cash rewards and talk knowingly of clubs who dole out enough 'boot money' to pay their stars' mortgages. I can only speak from my own experience: at Swansea the only cash to which we had access at the final whistle was the modest beer-kitty, sufficient for two or three pints apiece. On the other hand, I certainly never considered that Swansea men should have to pay for club stockings, shorts or jerseys when ten or twenty thousand customers were paying at the gate to watch them perform. Some English players used to point out earnestly to me how it cost them money to play rugby, and that this was the only true amateurism. Well, that is how it has to be if only a few dozen folk come through the turnstiles; and I am quite happy for my friends across the border to feel a warm moral glow as they fork out money for their kit or pay club subscriptions!

My young readers, finally, will have noticed the word 'beer' creeping into the story here and there. I will not mince words: beer is part of the rugby scene and its marvellous conviviality. Over the years 'J.P.R.' and myself, along with accomplished foreigners like Sandy Carmichael and Alan Old, have been exalted by various team-mates to high-ranking positions as trusted beer tasters.

But alcohol, though a good friend, is a bad task-master, and for three days before a big match not a drop passed my lips. From this chapter you will have gained an insight into the myriad small things which can upset and disturb the mood of men keyed up to give of their best in a most demanding sport: a hangover is something that everyone has it within his power to do without.

11 Wales and the World

David Parry-Jones

It has become the fashion for leading players to include in their memoirs a team selection or two, naming the contemporaries whom they feel were really outstanding. The great All Black Colin Meads did it recently, as did Willie John McBride, in the certain knowledge that their selections would start tongues wagging all over the rugby world — and Willie John made sure of that when, ignoring all the other great locks of the sixties and seventies, he put the name of Stan Meads next to that of brother Colin in his World XV.

So Mervyn Davies is going to follow suit, and later in this chapter he picks a World XV, composed (except in one instance) of International players against whom he competed, and a Wales team to oppose it. But before being allowed the luxury of behaving as a 'supremo', favouring some players and discarding others, and pronouncing upon their respective abilities and shortcomings, it is only fair that he himself should go under the spotlight for a period. Let us note, therefore, what critics and observers have said about him.

To begin on a lighter note, consider the reaction of the Old Guildfordians after Merv had played a couple of matches for them as a twenty-one-year-old in 1968. 'We had to drop him,' recalled chairman Ed Ram, 'because he didn't quite fit into our scheme of things!' He added, though, that the club swiftly recognised that their new number 8 was destined for greater heights, and were not too surprised when, soon after his departure for London Welsh, Merv began winning caps for Wales.

On the International field his long, lean build at first puzzled and

amused opponents and critics used to stockier, more broadly con-
structed physiques. Colin Meads summed him up as 'a Heath
Robinson contraption dressed up in rugby kit', while he reminded
John Reason of the *Daily Telegraph* of 'an undernourished hair-pin'.

Long before Merv's enforced retirement, however, both men had
changed their tune. Meads has written, 'If one of the 1971 Lions
more than any other spelled out from the start the trouble the All
Blacks would have in the series, it was Mervyn. . . . By controlling
possession at the end of the line-out he nullified a traditional New
Zealand strength.' John Reason considered that by 1975-6 he was
responsible for 'half the effectiveness' of the Welsh pack.

Returning briefly to 1971, one of the southern hemisphere's most
outspoken critics, Terry McLean, commented: 'Not many International players put as much conscientious effort into their game.
Mervyn tried to play his best in every match, and succeeded in doing just that a remarkable number of times.'

Once he had announced his decision to retire in 1976, Mervyn
Davies's contribution to the Welsh game was thoughtfully analysed
by many senior observers among his own countrymen. Said Wilfred
Wooller, 'He bound a scrummage, he pushed his weight, he
dominated a line-out; he cleaned up untidy play, he followed the
flankers like a shadow, he reached the outer perimeter of the
defence. All these things – and more – he did with consummate
ease.' That latter sentiment is echoed by the comment of R. C. C.
Thomas, another fine back-row player: 'There was an economy of
effort which belied his athleticism,' wrote Clem in the *Observer*
newspaper. 'He would unflinchingly kill any dangerous ball, his
tackling was definitive and match-winning, and he possessed great
courage.'

Thomas also remarked that Mervyn became a great and well-
loved leader, a point underlined by the former Wales stand-off half
Cliff Morgan. Leadership capacity, resilience, character and self-
discipline were the virtues which Cliff picked out, going on to
bracket the Welshman unhesitatingly with all-time greats in his position like Hennie Muller, Brian Lochore and Des O'Brien. Alun
Pask, previously the most-capped Welsh number 8, admits that
when his successor first appeared on the scene he had doubts about

his strength. 'By the end of 1969 those doubts had vanished,' says Pask. 'I came to realise that he was a very complete forward, with all the skills. To Welsh forward play Merv was what Gareth Edwards has been to the backs.'

What of the views held by Mervyn Davies's team-mates? John Taylor, a back-row colleague both at Old Deer Park and for Wales, says bluntly: 'It was like playing next to a tank.' Willie John McBride dubs him, 'That prince of number 8s.' Gareth Edwards is a bit more explicit: 'Playing with "Swerve" meant that someone like myself could afford to take risks, safe in the knowledge that if something went wrong he would be at hand to tidy up. He was the best forward in the world in my time – I count myself lucky to have played International rugby with, rather than against, him!'

Practically the only adverse judgment, therefore, that can be included to balance all the accolades bestowed upon the tall Welshman is his extraordinary omission from the Rothmans 'World Team of the Year' listed in their annual for 1974-5. It was picked with the combined votes of eight journalists from the International Board countries plus France, seven of whom named Andy Ripley as the leading number 8 forward of the day. The only vote cast for Mervyn Davies was that of the English contributor, who was debarred from naming a fellow countryman.

The sole comment that can be made is that the poll took place in the period immediately before the Lions' tour of South Africa when, by his own admission, Mervyn was not playing so well. Some faces in the Pressbox were presumably rather pink by the time the book was published in the autumn, after Ripley's challenge for a Test place had been ruthlessly overcome.

Let us leave the final summing-up to Carwyn James: 'Mervyn's personal style was based on an uncanny sense of positional play. He progressed quietly from the corner-flagging role of the traditional number 8 to the modern concept of going forward, winning possession and distributing well – though if the midfield was in need of help he always seemed to be nearby to provide it. More than any other player in the sixties and seventies, he influenced the development of a new back-row pattern.'

Si monumentum requiris, circumspice.

MERVYN DAVIES

Personally, I was seldom critical of the Welsh selectors during my career. I didn't have to be – they never dropped me!

However, the sound of gunfire is never far distant from their ears, which on the whole makes me glad that I have never seriously been involved in the business of choosing a national XV. Furthermore, the demands made upon their time, energy and enthusiasm are absolutely enormous. They may be VIPs during their term of office, basking in a lot of limelight, but they certainly pay for this in terms of endeavour.

That is one reason why I believe selectors need to be comparatively young men. More importantly, the speed of change in the rugby game demands that teams are picked by people who have not long been in retirement and are in touch with new trends. Thus in my last years I approved of the presence of Clive Rowlands, John Dawes and Keith Rowlands in the Welsh Big Five.

People sometimes ask me what is the right number of men to serve on a selection committee. At the time of writing England have seven, which I consider too many. It must surely breed deadlock and disagreement, with the result that an outstanding but controversial player may be passed over for a lesser one who is acceptable to all. On the other hand, sufficient selectors are needed to give wide geographic cover and watch a broad spectrum of candidates in action.

Occasionally there are calls for a single rugby 'supremo', enjoying the status of an Alf Ramsay or a Don Revie in England's Association Football set-up – I suggest that England's lack of soccer success gives an immediate lie to that one! But seriously, unless he has huge self-confidence amounting almost to arrogance, one man just cannot be sure enough of his perception and judgment to be certain of choosing the best available XV.

Agreed, a national team coach must have a place on his country's selection committee, and he may even be the dominant figure within it. But he requires both the opinions of colleagues to test his own ideas against, and the information they can supply on the form and potential of candidates whom he has been unable to watch. No, I conclude that the five-man system as operated by Wales is the best. It certainly produced the goods in my time – and Cliff Jones never tires of pointing out that since 1965 he has been instrumental in choosing four Triple Crown sides and two which won Grand Slams, which he claims as a personal selectorial record!

However, enough of theories and speculation. I propose to become a 'supremo' in this chapter and, assuming power without any responsibility whatsoever, indulge myself by selecting two teams of superstars drawn from the top players with and against whom I played. No doubt if they can meet each other one day in Valhalla they will draw a crowd of several million!

Since some excellent contemporaries will have to be omitted, I should emphasise that my choice will be dictated by the desire to choose XVs which would function smoothly as teams. As we shall see, for instance, I leave Phil Bennett out of my Wales side – and that hurts – but I shall opt for Barry John at stand-off because of his club partnership with Gareth Edwards at Cardiff. Let us, though, deal with the World XV first.

At full-back, taking the view that, all other things being equal, ability to counter-attack is vital, I go for the Frenchman Pierre Villepreux. Hiller and Kiernan I rule out because I think they were better suited to the old 'last line of defence' full-back game, while McCormick of New Zealand fails to make my side because of the way his game fell apart under the ultimate pressure as applied by Barry John at Dunedin in 1971. Villepreux, on the other hand, was both a model of dependability and a man you had to watch like a hawk for incursions into the line. He was a tremendous punter of the ball, too – it was shattering to be on the attack close to France's line only for Pierre to boot the ball back over one's head as far as the half-way line.

Although New Zealand is not noted for flair among her backs, I select Brian Williams on the right wing. A powerful runner, he was the All Blacks' main attacking weapon in my time and possessed a better temperament than his petulant little fellow countryman Grant Batty. The left wing I reserve for England's Dave Duckham, a magnificent sight in full cry for the line with his flowing blond locks and long-striding thighs. From ten yards' distance the huge

Duckham side-step looked obvious and predictable, but so often I saw it leave tacklers stranded and leaden-footed.

I regret (or perhaps I ought to be grateful as a Welshman!) that the true Duckham has seldom been seen in the British Isles, for it was his misfortune to hit a peak during a poor era of England rugby. When the ball reached him at Twickenham or Murrayfield Dave was often so startled that he scarcely knew what to do with it. But his performances for the Lions in New Zealand (when he stole the Test berth from John Bevan) leave me in no doubt at all of his qualifications for inclusion in top company.

At inside-centre, or second five-eighth as they would call him down under, I choose New Zealand's Ian MacRae. A strong runner, very hard to stop, Ian was the All Blacks' crash-ball specialist, whom very often it was my duty to stop. He would come hurtling back at an angle towards the set-piece; and once you had tackled him you knew that the arrival of the whole New Zealand pack was imminent, descending like a ton of bricks on the ruck he had set up. With him I pair Ireland's Mike Gibson, a complete antithesis to MacRae, and a man who could splinter defences and win matches on his own. In a changing-room, I never looked at Mike without marvelling that such a spare, thin man could be so brave and devastating in the tackle. A considerable thinker and tactician on the field, he was, therefore, a very complete footballer.

Having chosen him in the centre I find myself faced with a problem at stand-off half. One after another I was forced to eliminate men against whom I had played: Romeu? — too predictable. Burgess? — not consistent or adaptable enough. McGann? — useful but not world class. It would have been tempting to slot Phil Bennett in here, but since I am committed to choosing 'foreigners', I decided that I would have to break the rules and pick a man against whom I did not actually play but who greatly impressed me when I saw his performance against the Welsh back row in autumn 1976. Hugo Porta is his name, he is an Argentinian, and it would have been a grand challenge to confront him. Even from set-pieces he possessed the ability to make clean breaks (as Trevor Evans and Terry Cobner found to their cost); he revealed considerable tactical awareness; and he proved himself a fine kicker of the ball, with an eagle eye for a dropped-goal opportunity.

If relatively untested at the highest level, Hugo would be well looked-after by my inside-half, Sid Going. I choose him because, in short, he consistently presented me with more problems than any other scrum-half in the world. Immensely strong for his size, he loved taking on back-row forwards close to the scrum (did he invent the Maori side-step?), and since he was so compact I found difficulty in getting down to tackle him effectively. To beat New Zealand in my time you had to neutralise the Going threat, and it is a great compliment to reveal that he was the only individual opponent to deal with whom the 1971 Lions laid special plans. His non-stop chatter on the field used to irritate me: 'Aw, ref, give us a break,' when penalised for a crooked put-in; 'That so-and-so's yards offside,' pointing to an opposing flanker who was menacing him. But on reflection I find it amusing and the sign of a great competitor.

Turning to the props, I select (as I shall with my Welsh XV) men who were basically good scrummagers, but who brought something special to their game, raising it into the realm of greatness. Ian McLauchlan will be one choice, a man whom I did not rate as a Test prop until Carmichael and McLoughlin were savaged out of contention at Canterbury in 1971. But the 'Mouse' rose to the challenge. He worked hard on his technique, developing it to a high level of skill, and ended up by proving that short, squat props could see off taller, heavier opponents by correct posture. For Scotland, Ian hated being defeated and sometimes let it show, but I don't hold that against him, for I am sure that I did occasionally too. And it is to his credit that he scored one of the most important tries of my era, after charging down Alan Sutherland's mis-hit clearing kick in the first Test of the '71 series.

Along with him I pick Ken Gray, an outstanding member of the All Black pack against Wales in 1969. His propping was rock-steady and he was quick and agile around the field. Gray was more intelligent, too, than several of the men who succeeded him in New Zealand's front row. Between the props I select England's John Pullin, technically a superb hooker, whose clean striking pretty well guaranteed his side the ball on their put-in.

You could not leave Colin Meads out of any World XV chosen

from my contemporaries. Colin is a man who had nearly as many critics as friends in rugby circles, yet I salute him as an immense man, physically and mentally. When I tackled him, as I often did, I knew that I would have to hit him far harder than anyone else to make any impression on his progress. At set scrummages he was solid as concrete, at the line-out he won consistent ball without ever getting very high off the ground, in the open he could run like a three-quarter. I am sorry that it always fell to us to oppose each other; it would have been good to have him on my side.

With Colin I pair Walter Spanghero of France, a beautiful runner and ball-player (with the biggest hands I have ever seen) who epitomised all that was best in French forward play. Regrettably, my impressions of Frik du Preez as a lock for South Africa are a bit hazy, but perhaps that is a good reason for leaving him out.

I must admit, though, that I was tempted to pick two South Africans for my flank positions, Piet Greyling and Jan Ellis, men who worked supremely well in harness together. This would have involved omitting Ian Kirkpatrick, however, the best individual flanker I played against. So I choose Kirkie with Greyling, whose destructive capacities I rated very highly when I met him for London Counties, Wales and the Barbarians in 1970.

Finally, at number 8 I have to opt for Brian Lochore, from whom I learned such a lot as a newcomer to International rugby in 1969. A man of awe-inspiring stature, he was a worthy opponent at the tail of the line-out, besides being rather rapid around the open field. Because Brian was a magnificent captain, under whose control I readily place my World XV, he gets my vote over the big Frenchman Benoit Dauga.

I see that the inclusion of Kirkpatrick and Lochore means that their team contains a preponderance of New Zealanders. This simply reflects my often-expressed respect for their country's rugby footballers, and the fact that they were so successful against Wales in my time. For that reason, too, their presence would help to motivate the fifteen Welshmen I shall now select to oppose them.

As modestly as possible, I shall accept the number 8 position in the Welsh side for the perfectly logical reason that in my time no other man played there for Wales. My thirty-eight caps were won consecutively, so I have no option other than to pick myself!

For the same reason although Roger Blyth once stood in for him J. P. R. Williams is a 'must' at full-back. But there are a host of more important ones. For forwards, it was a fabulous sensation to know that John would always be in the right place doing the right thing, whether a Welsh attack was breaking down and needed support, whether an opponent had split the defence and had to be tackled to prevent a try, or whether the other side was kicking for position back over our heads.

His supreme confidence even made some of his team-mates lazy: so positive were we that J. P. R. could cope in a crisis that we sometimes omitted to chase back and lend him assistance. I cannot fault him — even recalling times when he put the cat among the pigeons by playing an occasional game as a flanker. Once we played in the same back row for Stanley's XV against Oxford University, and for a mere back he performed astonishingly well!

Gerald Davies, the most complete three-quarter I have ever seen, gets my invitation to appear on the right wing. Like Gibson he was a brave tackler for so slight a man, but 'Reames' was a more regular scorer of tries from seemingly impossible situations. A great quality appreciated by supporting forwards was that Gerald never died with the ball, always making it available to others if he could not break through himself. Finally, the entertainment value he represented for Cardiff, London Welsh and Wales was matchless.

For my left winger I go back to 1969 to pick Maurice Richards, who left our game abruptly to go north after Wales returned from her Australasian tour. John Williams was the fastest left wing of my time, though a bit short on subtlety; John Bevan combined size with guts, and scored tries that would have been beyond the capability of any rival; but Maurice had everything — physique, determination, speed, and a shattering side-step. I shall never forget the score he got for us against New Zealand in the second Test of 1969: having beaten McCormick with an inside feint and outside body-swerve that left the All Black rolling on his back, he still had the momentum to beat four other covering defenders and reach the corner flag.

I have indicated my high regard for John Dawes elsewhere, and have no hesitation in naming him as one of my centres. His leadership qualities made him the man I was most willing to play under, and I would ask him to captain the side. And because I know how good Dawes could make a partner look, I envy the person picked to play next to him.

Who shall it be? Jarrett? Arthur Lewis? Raybould? Bergiers? Fenwick? Ian Hall? Or Raymond Gravell? I go for the last named, because with a cool, deft centre like 'Sid' Wales can afford to have the block-busting approach of big Ray. I also take into account the Llanelli man's unsurpassed will to win, which gives him a slight edge over rivals.

As I remarked earlier, I cannot separate Barry and Gareth as my half-backs, and I seriously doubt whether a more complete pair of players has ever been seen on a rugby field. Both were men who drew upon themselves pressure from opposing defences, not only overcoming it brilliantly but also creating freedom and space which team-mates could use. I certainly benefited from this, like other Wales back-row forwards.

As an individual, my comment on Barry is that he was a joy to support, for he always got the ball across the advantage line somehow, and there is nothing forwards like better from backs than being nursed upfield. You had to keep him perpetually in your sights, for he was ever liable to do something totally unexpected. Because of the pleasure I took in tackling I was quite prepared to do some of his share for him, but I am not one of those who say that the 'King' could not tackle. The suicidal way in which he stopped a try by huge Benoit Dauga in the Paris Grand Slam match of 1971 is proof of his courage.

Gareth, whom I would select ahead of Sid Going in an all-comers' World XV, had a lot of the New Zealander's virtues, including a low centre of gravity, a razor-sharp nose for an opening close to the scrummage, and immense body strength, proportionately greater than my own, which took him through all but the highest quality tackling. Even if a break by Gareth did not yield him a try, he would have taken two defenders out of the game, so something was invariably 'on' for the rest of us. His reflexes were astonishingly quick, while in defence his presence amounted to an addition to a back row.

Such a glittering back-division would deserve the best possession that could possibly be won. To help ensure this at the scrummages I choose Denzil Williams and Graham Price. Why, however, do I overlook Glyn Shaw, Phil Llewellyn, Barry Llewelyn, John Lloyd or Charlie Faulkner? Because my two selected props brought an extra element to their game which lifted it into a different class. Denzil, a splendid 'senior citizen' in my early days, was a past-master of the support role at a line-out. He will not mind my writing that he was a great exponent of the barely legal! I recall once being in the number five jumping position, and remaining at the peak of my leap for the ball for what seemed like thirty whole seconds. On descending I turned to find the grinning face of Denzil immediately behind me, and realised that my shorts were exceedingly tight from 'lifter's cramp'!

Graham Price's try near the end of his debut game in Paris was out of this world, emphasising his enormous stamina and also a fact well known to anyone who has observed him in training – that he is as fast as some three-quarters. In the close exchanges Graham was a formidable ally and, all in all, during my time he was the closest thing Wales produced to New Zealand's Gray.

I hate leaving Charlie Faulkner out, but I do choose another Pontypool man as my hooker, Bobby Windsor. The major alternative choice would be Jeff Young, but he had an unfortunate tendency to fall foul of referees because he struck so fast. Although a powerful man, who could also play at prop, Jeff also lacked Bobby's bristling aggression, which was so valuable on the '74 Lions' tour. Even normally civilised Englishmen took the field like men possessed after an hour before the kick-off spent in Bobby's abrasive company.

There are four places to fill, and two of them are the most difficult selections I have to make: a pair of locks. Consider the candidates: Brian Price, Brian Thomas, Delme Thomas, Alan Martin, Geoff Wheel, Ian Robinson, Mike Roberts, Geoff Evans, and Derek Quinnell. On reflection this long list may be a pointer to the uncertainty that existed in my time about the 'power-house', compared with the small number of men who became automatic choices at half back or on the wing. So I must be careful.

I take Alan Martin as my top choice, for he was probably the most improved Welsh forward in my playing days. It is the normal practice to pick a strong, mauling-type player to go with someone like Alan, which would suggest Brian Thomas or Geoff Wheel. However, since my three front-row men are so highly skilled in tight play, I can afford the luxury of a second jumper, so I opt for Delme Thomas. Although not the tallest of men, Delme consistently got higher off the ground than anyone else, and he had a big-match temperament steeled by experience in the most testing situations.

Finally, whom to pick as the men to flank me in the back row? Again, I have to choose between two pairs of candidates: Dai Morris and John Taylor were with me for roughly the first half of my International career, while I ended my days for Wales in between Terry Cobner and Trevor Evans.

You could say that sentiment plays a part in my selection of 'Bas' Taylor and Morris the Shadow, for we appeared as a back-row unit a record eighteen times for our country. Dai and Bas were complete-ly complementary to each other. The former's aim was always to be where the ball was, the latter was a fine handler with enough speed to have been a three-quarter. Both were also wholly committed to attacking rugby, which meant that I could give more attention to the defensive role which was my forte. So they were great to play alongside. Some people used to argue that they were too short for the modern back-row game, a taunt that used to infuriate John – es-pecially if he heard Scottish commentator Bill McLaren referring to him as 'wee John Taylor'! 'I'm all of six feet,' he would insist, draw-ing himself up to his full height. And often, at the tail of the line-out, I would get a sharp push in the back as 'Bas' made room for himself to get airborne and secure good possession.

All this does not mean that I am blind to the virtues of Terry Cobner, expert at tackling and turning a victim so that supporting forwards could obtain the ball, Trevor Evans and Tom David with their huge zest for conflict, or Dennis Hughes, one of the fittest of men. But, like Phil Bennett, they have to make room for a partnership that was tried and tested.

All told, that makes a pretty potent combination, one which I would take to beat the World XV – unless we lent them a Welsh coach to redress the balance! By the way, adhering to my firm belief that goal-kicking is of primary importance at the highest level, I have managed to include three dependable performers with the boot in Barry John, Alan Martin and John Taylor, with Gareth Edwards to fall back on in emergency.

My job, then, is done – let the arguments begin! And they will be endless, for one of the pleasures of these theoretical exercises is that there is absolutely no way of deciding their outcome. I do know one thing, though: a match between the two sides I have picked would illustrate and highlight every glorious aspect of a team-game which in my view is second to none. And when I take a look at the assembled names, I feel a glow of pride that my own rugby was played in such illustrious company.

WALES		THE WORLD
John P. R. Williams (London Welsh)	15	Pierre Villepreux (France)
Gerald Davies (Cardiff)	14	Brian Williams (New Zealand)
Raymond Gravell (Llanelli)	13	Ian MacRae (New Zealand)
John Dawes – captain (London Welsh)	12	Mike Gibson (Ireland)
Maurice Richards (Cardiff)	11	Dave Duckham (England)
Barry John (Cardiff)	10	Hugo Porta (Argentine)
Gareth Edwards (Cardiff)	9	Sid Going (New Zealand)
Graham Price (Pontypool)	1	Ian McLauchlan (Scotland)
Bobby Windsor (Pontypool)	2	John Pullin (England)
Denzil Williams (Ebbw Vale)	3	Ken Gray (New Zealand)
Delme Thomas (Llanelli)	4	Colin Meads (New Zealand)
Alan Martin (Aberavon)	5	Walter Spanghero (France)
Dai Morris (Neath)	6	Piet Greyling (South Africa)
Mervyn Davies (Swansea)	8	Brian Lochore – captain (New Zealand)
John Taylor (London Welsh)	7	Ian Kirkpatrick (New Zealand)

Final Whistle

David Parry-Jones

You do not spend upwards of sixty hours in someone's company without forming clear views on his character. My role as catalyst for Mervyn Davies's career reflections and recollections afforded a unique insight into the make-up of a man whose supreme ability at the rugby game meant that he had to learn to live with stardom.

The key to much of his personality lies in the oft-reiterated basis of his rugby philosophy: 'The elimination of errors from my play.' Errors make you look foolish; and Merv, it seems to me, has a well-developed antipathy towards appearing less than competent or at a loss. For this reason he is more sensitive than many realise about the slight limp which is one consequence of his illness. Most observers, if they noticed anything at all, would probably comment that he walks with a loose, loping gait; but Merv the perfectionist insists that it is a limp he carries.

Whether the limp, the slightly blurred vision and the inability to smell will right themselves in time is anybody's guess. On the whole Mervyn seldom alludes to his brain haemorrhage and his period as an invalid – and why should he? It is a traumatic experience for a fit young man at the height of his powers to be brought up sharply against the realities of existence and to realise suddenly that he is only human after all. But he will admit that some mornings, when he applies the razor to bristling stubble, he remembers the other blade that snipped away within his head and saved his life.

His reluctance to lose face means that in conversation he eschews snap-judgments, preferring to weigh words carefully before committing himself. He holds strong opinions, but in his pre-captaincy days, as a rather retiring member of the Welsh XV, he was rarely pressured into voicing them publicly. Command status on the field and off it demanded that he learned to articulate his views, which he now does with authority. He sees life chiefly in black and white, with no grey areas, which must have made for crisp, clearly defined leadership in the nine games when he skippered Wales, leaving team-mates in no doubt as to what was required of them.

He does not suffer fools gladly, and can be brusque and short with uninformed hangers-on who try to illuminate the finer points of rugby football for his benefit. But his patience with young admirers is considerable, and he well knows the value of a quip to steady the nerves of trembling autograph-hunters.

If we are drawing a warts-and-all sketch of Mervyn Davies, the sole blemish worth pointing out is an element of complacency. We were once discussing the use of spikes in training to achieve an extra yard of pace around the field, on which Merv was not exactly a greyhound. He blinked, before replying candidly that the idea had not occurred to him. Like most great performers, he was more conscious of the plus-factors in his game, and the means of exploiting them, than of any minor shortcomings. Perhaps an innate laziness had something to do with this, for by his own confession he is not the world's most energetic fellow! It might be most accurate to describe him as easy-going.

Although there was and is tremendous self-assurance incorporated in that large, powerful frame, it rarely if ever spills over into conceit. When he looks back at the way he played the number 8 game and the reasons why he became pre-eminent at it, he tends to seek refuge in under-statement: 'I simply did my job as effectively as possible.' That meant more effectively than anyone else.

All these characteristics made him, eventually, a superb dictator and controller of events in the playing arena. The fierce, almost hysterical debate in Wales over who should succeed him at number 8 (and who should inherit the captaincy) demonstrated beyond doubt how much his giant presence would be missed.

MERVYN DAVIES

Members of the older generation still tell me, 'You were pretty good, Merv. But your father was better.'

By now, whether spoken in jest or not, the gibe bounces off a skin thickened by nearly a decade in the public eye. It is nice to hear one's father paid a compliment; but equally, I am well satisfied with my own achievements in rugby football, and the record books are there to be consulted if necessary. Anyway, comparisons are odious, especially in a game which has changed so much not only since 1946 but also since 1966.

However, sons do get compared with fathers, whose shadows often stretch a long way down the years. As our youngster Christopher grows up and tries out the various sports and pastimes that are available to a healthy, energetic boy I shall be watching him much more carefully than he will realise. No doubt he will want to have a go at rugby, and that will please me — as long as no one attempts to throw him into it at too early an age. Not until they are thirteen and on the threshold of puberty, it seems to me, are boys able to cope with the pain and discomforts that rugby involves compared with, say, soccer. A harsh blow to the face, or a shin-bone raked by an over-zealous stud, can scar the mind of a child for years and perhaps put him off a game for good, but once he is into his teens a youngster starts to be able to absorb bumps and bruises. The immediate desire to shed tears gives way to a gritting of the teeth and a dawning understanding of the meaning of courage and endurance. Looking back to my own childhood, I think it was at that age that I also began to develop competitive aspirations, and the will to win which can often divide players of equal skill and ability in later years.

Christopher and his generation will no doubt be tempted by the mini-rugby idea, which has penetrated many junior schools in South Wales and which is specially designed to suit boys of nine to eleven years of age. It is supposed to be a counter-attraction to soccer, which can be played by as few as two participants in virtually any conditions and circumstances, and is an easy game for young minds to grasp and understand. However, I am quite happy for boys to potter around with soccer until they enter secondary school, when they may be profitably introduced to a game which will make more demands upon their skill, intellect and character.

And then? Should a son of mine turn against rugby, fair enough.

He must not feel that because his father played a bit then he also is obliged to try and excel at the game. I would rather he became a tiddly-winks International than feel he was wasting time on a sport with which he was out of sympathy, while his father cringed on the touch-line wondering why junior was failing to make the grade.

But if Christopher chooses rugby of his own free will, that will be a different matter. Then he will find me more than ready to tell him about the immense rewards the game has to offer those who are prepared to put something into it. To begin with, its aesthetic delights: the exuberant feeling of running with the ball, especially if you have ripped it from an opponent's hands first. The pleasure afforded by a hard, perfectly executed tackle, where bravery was needed to get in really low and avoid the flailing heels of the victim. The satisfaction of a well-timed leap at the line-out, with the ball clawed from the stretched fingers of a rival. The grim confidence forwards gain at the afternoon's first scrummage when an opposing eight retreats a foot or two. And the virtuous glow felt in the shower-room when you examine a large, purpling bruise and say to yourself, 'I remember getting it, but after that I didn't let it bother me.'

I can tell, too, of rugby's cameraderie – and I have a bound volume to prove my point! In autumn 1976 Thames Television inveigled me into a 'This Is Your Life' appearance, much to my chagrin in some ways, I must admit. Just two weeks before the recording I remember saying to a friend during casual conversation that in no way would Merv the Swerve submit to so embarrassing, tear-jerking an extravaganza! Then came an evening when I made a guest appearance on stage, along with fellow Internationals Gareth Edwards and Dewi Bebb, at a Max Boyce concert in Swansea – and sure enough from behind a curtain stepped the smooth-talking Eamonn Andrews. A quick glance at the faces of the others left me in no doubt that I was his quarry, and my initial reaction was one of extreme annoyance: 'They've damn well caught me!' I said angrily to myself.

Reluctantly, I decided to sit it out in order not to disappoint those who had set up the programme. Not much of the recording sticks in my mind (and I saw only five minutes of the subsequent transmission, since on the night I was helping to open a new club-house for Dinas Powys RFC). But I regretted that I had no control over the guest-list, with the result that some people who are very important to me were excluded, including Christopher; agreed, it was past his bed-time, but I thought they might have shot a few frames of film of him at our house. All told, it seemed to be an unwarranted intrusion into my privacy, and I found it hard to shed the feeling of having been duped. Even Shirley had sat on the secret for four whole months: her ability to remain mum was a revelation to me!

In spite of all that, however, the evening was undeniably memorable, partly through the appearance of Colin Meads, my old New Zealand friend and rival, who had taken precious time off from his King Country farm to fly 12,000 miles and bring his land's greetings to me. My jaw dropped when he joined the gathering, and I felt tremendously moved. Equally, it was grand to see Benoit Dauga from France, not long recovered from an accident as serious in its way as my own illness. Though an Irish contingent including Willie John McBride, who were all set to come, were frustrated by fog at Dublin Airport, Tom Grace and Mick Hipwell, who had been playing for Leinster in France, did drop in *en route* for home to link up with Englishmen, Scots and a sprinkling of my fellow countrymen. All of this proves that rugby men do not forget, and that friendships forged on the field and in the club-house afterwards are lasting ones. After the show everyone repaired to the nearby Dragon Hotel to eat, drink and gossip our way into the early hours. Here again I experienced an almost tangible tide of affection, as 'Pine Tree' Meads told me of the anxiety and concern with which New Zealanders had followed reports of my hospitalisation and convalescence.

Of course rugby football has now established itself as a world game, so that it is perhaps less surprising that the life and times of its major figures make world headlines. For yet another new trend during my time as a player was the increased number of short tours to or from Europe, bringing the old-established countries into contact with rugby's emergent nations. Canada, Japan, Tonga, Fiji and the Argentine have all had opportunities to play against Wales since

1970, while I have listened with interest to club players who have visited the USA and can speak with authority about the way the game is catching on there.

As a result of this intensified international to-ing and fro-ing my contemporaries and I have had our breadth of vision and understanding of other people's life-styles widened immeasurably, and have travelled far more widely than most other young men. The labels on my suitcases and hold-alls on top of the wardrobe tell the tale: Hong Kong, Tokyo, Dunedin, Ottawa, Pretoria, Sri Lanka, Singapore — thanks to my ability on the field I have been able to see them all.

Although touring was invariably fun, there was usually a more serious side. In Japan and Canada, for example, Wales were bent on expounding the rugby gospel, and demonstrating as well as we could to untutored eyes what a superb spectacle and experience the game can be at its best. We were criticised for fielding very strong sides in Tokyo and Osaka and winning by gigantic margins, but our heavy scoring showed the Japanese where they stood in the game and what they had to do in order to ascend into its higher echelons.

The Japanese visit of 1975 also yielded Wales a bonus, in that we came straight home to win a Grand Slam. Living and playing together for three weeks was good for my men, who developed an affinity that was truly reminiscent of club spirit. In fairness to our hosts, they brought home to us the point that rugby is a game where innovations are always possible and initiative is rewarded. We saluted the consideration that they had given to overcoming their biggest problem, lack of weight and height. They abbreviated the line-outs on their throw-in, and whisked the ball into the set-scrums with a minimum of delay, to cut down the amount of time spent shoving against bigger, more powerful opponents.

Cultural and social differences inevitably showed up on occasions. Japanese minds seem to work very rigidly, and the authorities had mapped out a time-table for us which left the boys little free time. Tourists are perfectly willing to show the flag and attend official functions, so long as time is also allowed to take it easy and forget about being on best behaviour. So coach John Dawes, manager Les Spence and myself, as captain, had to sit down and reschedule our movements. 'Shiggy' Konno, Japan's 'Mr Rugby' who, as far as I can see, runs the game almost single-handed east of Suez and north of Brisbane, was somewhat put out at first, but soon came to see our point of view.

Often on a tour a young man benefits by coming into contact with a senior member of the party, and I certainly valued the presence of Les Spence as our manager. He was a well-organised 'elder', whom I admired for his readiness to fraternise easily and amicably with his hosts, a nation whose prisoner-of-war he had been thirty years earlier. Les was the soul of good-mannered diplomacy, and socially the smattering of Japanese he had picked up as a PoW stood him in good stead. Indeed, the boys decided that occasionally his Japanese was more fluent than his English – as on the evening when he announced to the assembled gathering, 'Now I would like to introduce to you the Welsh coach, Don Jawes'! (He capped this in Cardiff later that autumn at a reception given to the Wallabies under their captain Garrick Fay, proclaiming: 'We say farewell and *bon voyage* to the popular Australians and Gay Farrick'!) A splendid tour companion, though, and a man who could be strict or completely informal as the occasion demanded.

In Japan women play a very secondary role in a man's world, and post-match functions were male-dominated. Though the bachelors in our party regretted this, we took the chance to introduce our hosts to a few traditional rugby songs. I believe we left them with the idea that although the game is important for eighty minutes, socialising in a lively – and sometimes earthy! – manner is an integral part of rugby in Wales. It was clear on the Canadian tour two years earlier that the New World appreciated this point, for many of their players were first-generation immigrants. On the other hand they were not as realistic as the Japanese about the game itself. Their noses were really put out of joint when Wales ran up totals of 60, 70 or 80 against the provinces and the national XV.

But I have high hopes for the future of rugby union football in Canada, for the following reason in particular. Clearly Canadians enjoy a tough, physical game like ours, as is evinced by their enthusiasm for Canadian Rules or grid-iron football within the schools. Here is the crucial point: once a boy leaves school he either makes it as a professional or turns his back on the game forever and enters a sporting void: there is no amateur system in which a man may participate during his twenties. The Canadian rugby union authorities can see a great opportunity here to make converts, so that we may witness some startling progress in North America during the next decade. The main problem they have to overcome in welding a national outlook and a national XV is distance. For Newfoundland to meet British Columbia means travelling more than 3000 miles, or further than Wales would have to fly to play Canada in Toronto.

Some final observations on the new nations who are crowding on to the big rugby circuit: sooner or later the great debate will have to be faced – do we attempt to maintain a European ethos in the game, or will we be forced to welcome the Argentinas and the Rumanias into rugby's corridors of power? Does our International Board see itself as the custodian of rugby's ark of the covenant for eternity, risking the breaking away of splinter groups from the New World and elsewhere who will seek to adjust the game to their needs and requirements? Or will the nations of north-west Europe, plus the former dominions of the southern hemisphere, admit that Fiji, Tonga, Japan and the rest have something to contribute and must be brought into the administrative levels of rugby football?

I do not know the answers to these problems. Instinctively, though, I feel that Wales and the older-established nations will have to face them soon. My country's Test match against the Pumas in October 1976 provided as stern an ordeal as we have endured at the hands of England in recent years; how can we say, 'Well done, Argentina – but you must remain second-class rugby citizens'? South Africa is not at present a favoured nation as far as sporting contact is concerned: may not the newcomers from Latin America be suitable successors to her on the International Board? I shall watch the developing debate with interest, and may have something to toss into it.

Below the administrative level, Wales can feel proud of the contribution she has made to the nurturing of the game outside Europe. Each year students from the four corners of the globe crowd into Aberystwyth for courses run by the WRU's Coaching Organiser,

Ray Williams, and return to their own countries that bit more enlightened. I only hope this broadcasting of Welsh rugby know-how will not result in too many untoward reverses for us in years to come!

We have been talking about beginners; I was fortunate to spend my playing career in what amounted to a university of rugby, the Welsh club and International scene. And it so happened that most of my days on the field were spent in the company of supremely gifted colleagues. That was a thought uppermost in my mind when I visited Buckingham Palace in November 1976 to be invested with my Order of the British Empire Medal.

Some Welshmen, it is rumoured, have declined royal recognition for one reason or another: that is their business. Personally, when I received the prime minister's letter asking if I would accept an OBE I had no hesitation at all. For a start I am something of a royalist at heart, an admirer of the royal family for the hard work they put in, for the civilised example they set, and for the continuity they give to our ruling tradition. So when Shirley, Dyfrig and I left Pontlliw for London one Wednesday morning in a limousine lent by my good friend Brian Lewis of Howells Garages in Cardiff, I was more keyed up than I cared to admit.

Eric Morecambe and Ernie Wise joked and gagged their way down the long corridor in which we recipients queued before entering the state-room, and the audience gave an unheard-of titter when the pair tried to get in step as they approached Her Majesty to the strains of 'Give me Sunshine'. Nonetheless the tension was high, and I was so anxious to do everything according to the book when my turn came that I completely failed to register any lasting impression of the great moment.

Apart from the fact that she was shorter than I had expected, my abiding recollection of the thirty seconds I spent with the Queen was that she recognised me (I put that down to my height) and was able to enquire about my state of health. 'I'm about ninety-nine per cent recovered,' I replied, remembering after a second or two to add 'Ma'am'. Was I still involved in rugby football, she wanted to know, whereupon I explained that I was now writing and broadcasting on the game. Then it was all over, and I was bowing and retreating to sit and watch the remainder of the ceremony.

The point was, I believe, that the total Welsh achievement during the previous eighteen months had earned me my medal, and I accepted it as an honour bestowed upon my team. The medal is mine; the glory is shared by Bobby, Trevor, Gareth, 'Benny', 'Reames' and the others. And I am glad and proud that, by her gesture, the Queen focused the gaze of the whole United Kingdom upon a very special Welsh achievement.

On our exit into the Palace forecourt the Press photographers had Shirley, Dyfrig and me hopping around like dancing guinea-pigs, and we were grateful for the presence of Eric and Ernie to take off some of the pressure. The former had indulged in some sleight of hand, with the result that when he opened his presentation case before the cameras it was seen to contain his wrist-watch. Pretending to look horrified, Eric complained that Buckingham Palace was the last place on earth where he expected to experience such duplicity!

After the excitement we retired to the Wig and Pen, a pleasant Fleet Street tavern where old friends in John Taylor and John (OBE) Dawes joined us for a few drinks. Chris Lander of the *Daily Mirror* arrived to stand another round or two, and in the end the party from South Wales were relieved to be chauffeur-driven back down the M4.

Distinction, then — the final accolade that the rugby game can bestow upon its favourite sons. Truly, everything came my way, and I cannot say that I regret a single moment of the time spent on the field playing with the oval ball. Indeed, I cannot imagine what I would have done with my leisure time in other circumstances.

I must also acknowledge the game's therapeutic value, for it represents a magnificent opportunity to rid oneself of the pent-up frustrations and irritations of a week's work. Whether early on as a schoolmaster or later as a business representative I never felt so relaxed as in the post-match winding-down period at Old Deer Park or St Helens. For, even in apparently easy-going men, there lurk not far below the surface bellicose and brutal instincts and tendencies; after a grim forward tussle lasting eighty minutes I used to feel that the aggressive side of my nature had been given its head, and that the conflicting sides of my personality were, for a while, at peace.

Some critics say, 'It is ridiculous to take it all so seriously. Rugby is only a game.' They are guilty of a failure of understanding: of course it is just a game, and that is how the top performers see it. My contemporaries were men who gave total concentration and commitment to their sport on the field. Thereafter it was kept in perspective, as no more than a thoroughly absorbing pastime. It is others who complain that rugby is too close to a religion in Wales and that the top players are like gods. This is nonsense to anyone who really knows the scene! International and leading club players try to keep things on a realistic level. How, otherwise, could we smile in defeat? If our admirers wish to lionise us, that is their affair. Perhaps, since the latter half of this twentieth century is short on heroes, our victories, our feats, our abilities satisfy a genuine craving.

And now I, too, am a spectator. Often I itch to be back in action, especially when I see a player whose supremacy cries out for a tough, ruthless challenge of the kind I could once provide. At other times – perhaps on a bitter December afternoon with freezing fog hovering just above bleary floodlights – I tell myself that I must have been slightly insane to engage in a sport where a boot on the knee-cap, knuckles in the mouth or an elbow in the ribs can ruin an otherwise carefree week-end.

But my attitude doesn't really matter. The game will go on without me. When Kirkpatrick, Fouroux, Irvine, Gibson, Duckham and Edwards have hung up their boots, other great players will step from the wings. And Wales will find other number 8 forwards, too.

And yet . . . it would be agreeable, just one more time, to crunch Ray Gravell to the ground on his crash-ball burst for Llanelli. Or even to be systematically done over by the Pontypool front row – before struggling upright to carry the battle back to them!